Navigating
the New
Evangelization

Navigating the New Evangelization

Raniero Cantalamessa, OFM Cap.

Foreword by Bishop Christopher Coyne, SLD

Pauline
BOOKS & MEDIA

Library of Congress Cataloging-in-Publication Data

Cantalamessa, Raniero.

[Come la scia di un vascello. English]

Navigating the new evangelization / Raniero Cantalamessa, OFM Cap. ; Foreword by Bishop Christopher Coyne, SLD.

pages cm

ISBN-13: 978-0-8198-5182-6

ISBN-10: 0-8198-5182-5

1. Evangelistic work--History. I. Title.

BV3770.C3613 2014

266'.2--dc23

2013031112

Originally published by Edizioni San Paolo, Milan in Italian as *Come la Scia di Un Vascello: Orizzonti per Una Nuova Evangelizzazione,* copyright © by Edizioni San Paolo s.r.l. — Cinisello Balsamo (MI). Author Raniero Cantalamessa.

Translated by Bret Thoman

Unless otherwise noted, the Scripture quotations contained herein are from the *New Revised Standard Version Bible: Catholic Edition,* copyright © 1989, 1993, Division of Christian Education of the National Council of the Churches of Christ in the United States of America. Used by permission. All rights reserved.

Excerpts from *St. Francis of Assisi Writings and Early Biographies: English Omnibus of the Sources for the Life of St. Francis,* copyright ©1983 by the Franciscan Herald Press. Used with permission.

Excerpts from *The Letters and Diaries of John Henry Cardinal Newman: Vol. XXIV: A Grammar of Assent. January 1868 to December 1869* edited at the Birmingham Oratory with notes and an introduction by Charles Stephen Dessain and Thomas Gornall (1973) 145w. By permission of Oxford University Press.

Cover design by Rosana Usselmann

Cover photo: © istockphoto.com/Pieio, AIMSTOCK

Published by Pauline Books & Media, 50 Saint Pauls Avenue, Boston, MA 02130-3491. www.pauline.org

Printed in the U.S.A.

Pauline Books & Media is the publishing house of the Daughters of St. Paul, an international congregation of women religious serving the Church with the communications media.

1 2 3 4 5 6 7 8 9   18 17 16 15 14

Contents

Foreword

"Talk about Jesus. Talk about Jesus. Talk about Jesus." Whenever a person asks, "How do I evangelize? How do I spread the Good News?" I give that simple answer.

Evangelizing is first and foremost engaging someone in conversing about the Person, Jesus Christ: what he means to you as your Lord and Savior, what he means to others as Lord and Savior, and what he means to the world as its Lord and Savior. As simple as this is, we complicate the work of evangelization. We often imitate Naaman, the Syrian general who is told by the Prophet Elisha to bathe in the River Jordan seven times and his leprosy will be cured. At first Naaman reacts in anger because it is too simple, too easy: "Is that all I need to do? I have leprosy! It should take more than that!" When convinced by his servant to try it, Naaman bathes in the river seven times and is cured (see 2 Kgs 5).

The work of evangelization is rooted in the Person of Jesus Christ. It is a work that has been an explicit part of the Church's mission since its very foundation:

> And Jesus came and said to them, "All authority in heaven and on earth has been given to me. Go therefore and make disciples of all nations, baptizing them in the name of the

Father and of the Son and of the Holy Spirit, and teaching them to obey everything that I have commanded you. And remember, I am with you always, to the end of the age." (Mt 28:18–20)

As the Apostolic ministry unfolded after Pentecost, the Spirit-filled Saint Peter proclaimed:

Peter said to them, "Repent, and be baptized every one of you in the name of Jesus Christ so that your sins may be forgiven; and you will receive the gift of the Holy Spirit. . . ." So those who welcomed his message were baptized, and that day about three thousand persons were added. (Acts 2:38, 41)

This mission continues today wherever the Church proclaims the Good News to anyone who has not heard of the name of Jesus. For a number of years, however, we have been hearing a call to embrace the new evangelization, an effort on the part of the Church to re-evangelize those peoples and countries that were Catholic in the past but are no longer living the ardor or fire of Catholic Christianity. The new evangelization means that we can no longer assume that countries, societies, and individuals in the West are guided by Judeo-Christian values or faith. It is a call to us in the West to proclaim the Good News anew: at work, at play, over our backyard fences, wherever we may be in daily conversing and living.

As a Catholic bishop, I have had many opportunities to converse with others who are undertaking this work within the Church: fellow bishops, priests, deacons, religious, teachers, parish and diocesan evangelizers, laymen and laywomen who are excited about spreading the Good News. While much of this conversation has been about the "how" of the new evangelization, especially as it involves evangelization within and through the digital culture (video, Internet, texting, and so on), it seems to me that the "what" of evangelization is primary:

What is it we are trying to do, and what is it we are trying to convey in the new evangelization? The new as well as the old means of communication are there for the Church to use as empty vessels waiting to be filled. We do not have to invent the means. What we have to do is focus the content from "what" to "Who"—the Person, Jesus Christ, and then, with the Holy Spirit's grace, to help people connect with Jesus.

Father Raniero Cantalamessa, OFM Cap., does this New Evangelizing work very well. I first encountered his writings when I was a seminarian in the 1980s and then as a graduate student-priest in Rome in the early 1990s. Father Cantalamessa has served as Preacher of the Papal Household since 1980, offering retreats and spiritual reflections to the Pope and the Roman Curia every Friday in Lent and Advent. Because Father Cantalamessa is the only priest who preaches to the Pope, you can well imagine the talent, skill, and holiness necessary for such a ministry. As a seminarian and then a priest, I found Father Cantalamessa's homilies a rich source of spiritual sustenance and thought. Even now as a bishop, I find myself taking one of his books from the bookshelf for a good spiritual read and an exercise in Italian, although I have some in an English translation as well.

You will find Father Cantalamessa's writing conversational in style, expressing thoughts that are accessible and clear. He writes as if he is talking to a room full of friends, sprinkling his writings with quotes from numerous sources: Scripture, the Fathers of the Church, the later saints and Doctors of the Church, theologians, poets, thinkers, and authors—and stories and anecdotes intended to clarify the teaching at hand. Saint Augustine, in his treatise *On the Teaching of Christian Doctrine*, said that a catechist (a teacher of Christian faith and living) must "teach, please, and persuade." I contend that Father

Cantalamessa has done just that in his edifying writing on the new evangelization.

As I already mentioned, I have had the opportunity to converse with men and women who are engaged in the work of the new evangelization. They come from many different places and cultures and offer many different insights and much advice on this pressing pastoral endeavor. From this has come a realization that, while there is much that we have in common throughout the universal Church, the new evangelization recognizes the uniqueness that geography, language, and culture bring to life and to faith-living. While Father Cantalamessa is rooted in a European culture and milieu, much of what he writes is as true for the Church in the United States as it is for the Church in Europe—and elsewhere for that matter. The focus of the new evangelization is the *kerygma*, that is, the proclaiming of the Good News that is ordered to a relationship with Jesus that he makes possible, together with his call to daily repentance and conversion. This kerygma, this work of the new evangelization, is done the world over in particular places and cultures. While Jesus is "the same yesterday and today and forever" (Heb 13:8), *how* Jesus is proclaimed must take into account the culture and land. Thus, an American Catholic reader not only will find oneself stirred by Father Cantalamessa's insights on the new evangelization, but also must ask how these insights apply to the people and culture of the United States.

Readers of this book, interested in advancing the work of the new evangelization, will find much to ponder as Father Cantalamessa draws essential direction from the *Parable of the Sower*:

> This parable, in and of itself, tells us that the essential reason for the success of the Christian mission does not come from outside but from within. It is not the work of the sower, or

even principally of the land, but of the seed. The seed cannot sow itself on its own, yet it sprouts automatically and of itself. After having sown the seed, the sower can even go to sleep, for the life of the seed no longer depends on him. When this seed is the seed that "falls into the earth and dies," that is, Jesus Christ, nothing can prevent it from bearing much fruit (see Jn 12:24). People can give all the explanations they want for this fruit, but those will always remain superficial and will never arrive at the essential (see page 7).

For Father Cantalamessa, the Parable sounds a caution: "the effort of the new evangelization faces two dangers: one is inertia, laziness, not doing anything and letting others do all the work; the other is launching into many busy but ultimately empty human activities" (see page 24).

I invite the reader to experience this book as a summons calling one and all from laziness and indifference into engagement and contemplation. There are many "seeds" of Christ that, when carefully watered and fed by the power of the Holy Spirit, will implant in our hearts so that each of us may bring forth a harvest of plenty to the glory of God the Father.

BISHOP CHRISTOPHER J. COYNE, SLD
Vicar General
Archdiocese of Indianapolis

Preface

This book* brings together the meditations given at the Papal Household of Pope Benedict XVI during Advent 2010 and 2011. I hope these meditations will serve as a small contribution to the work of re-evangelizing the secularized world, a work that requires all the Church's efforts.

In chapters 1 through 4 (meditations preached in Advent 2011†), four examples are identified in which one can see an increase or a renewal of missionary activity, namely:

1. The first three centuries of Christian history, in particular, the second half of the third century when large parts of the Roman Empire were converted. Protagonists: the bishops;

2. The fourth to the ninth centuries, in which we witness the re-evangelization of Europe after the barbarian invasions. Protagonists: the monks;

---

* Originally published in Italian as *Come la scia di un vascello: Orrizzonti per una nuova evangelizzazione* (*In the Wake of a Great Ship: Horizons for a New Evangelization*). *Ed.*

† These meditations are found in the first part of the book although they were preached after those of 2010. *Ed.*

3. The sixteenth century, with the discovery of the inhabitants of the New World and their conversion to Christianity. Protagonists: the friars;

4. The current era, which sees the Church engaged in re-evangelizing the secularized West. Protagonists: the laity.

In each of these cases, we can try to discern the mistakes to avoid and the examples to imitate. In addition, we should note the specific contributions to evangelization that should be made by pastors, those in monastic life, those in active religious life, and the laity.

In chapters 5 through 7 (meditations preached in Advent 2010), we continue to reflect on evangelization in the current age by examining some of the major challenges that the proclamation of the Gospel encounters in today's world: atheistic scientism, rationalism, and secularism. We shall bring to light the response that the Christian faith allows us to give to each of them—all in a spirit of dialogue, not of polemics. We follow the First Letter of Peter, which exhorts Christians to give a reason for the hope that is in them, but "with gentleness and reverence" (see 1 Pt 3:15ff.).

Some terminology used in this book is inspired by an image of Charles Péguy, who speaks of Christian prayer metaphorically as the wake of a great ship that begins with a point—the two hands of Jesus joined—and gradually broadens until it is lost in the horizon. Here the image is applied to the preaching of the Church, which also began with a point—the proclamation of Jesus—and developed over time and space, leading to the richness of today's doctrine, laws, and institutions. But it has to start over again from that point.

CHAPTER I

Go into All the World

⳨

The first wave
of evangelization

1. The spread of Christianity in the first three centuries

Let us begin with a reflection on Christian evangelization in the first three centuries. One reason in particular makes this era the model for all time: it was when Christianity expanded exclusively due to its own force. No "secular arm" was supporting it, nor were conversions due to some external, material, or cultural benefit. Becoming Christian was not a custom or a fad but a countercultural choice, often made at the risk of one's life. In some ways, the same situation is now repeating itself in various parts of the world.

The Christian faith was born with universal openness. Jesus told his apostles to go "into all the world" (Mk 16:15), to "make disciples of all nations" (Mt 28:19), to be his witnesses "to the ends of the earth" (Acts 1:8), to preach to all nations the "repentance and forgiveness of sins" (Lk 24:47).

This universality was already taking hold in principle during the apostolic generation, although not without difficulty or struggle. On the day of Pentecost, the first barrier was overcome—that of ethnicity (the three thousand converts belonged to different races, but they were all Jewish believers). In the house of Cornelius and in the so-called Council of Jerusalem, the most difficult barrier of all was overcome (mostly due to Paul's prodding)—the religious barrier that divided Jews from Gentiles. The Gospel now had before it the entire world, even if, at that time, the then-known world was limited to the Mediterranean Basin and the confines of the Roman Empire.

It is more difficult to follow the actual, or geographical, expansion of Christianity in the first three centuries. But that is not necessary for our purposes. The most comprehensive study, still unsurpassed in this regard, is *The Mission and Expansion of Christianity in the First Three Centuries* by Adolf von Harnack.[1]

A dynamic increase in the missionary activity of the Church took place when Commodus was Roman emperor (180–192), and also in the second half of the third century, that is, until the eve of the great persecution of Diocletian in 302. Apart from some sporadic local persecutions, this was a period of relative peace that allowed the nascent Church to consolidate and develop a new type of missionary activity.

Let's examine this innovation. In the first two centuries, the propagation of the faith was entrusted to personal initiative. Itinerant prophets, mentioned in the *Didache*,* traveled from place to place. Many conversions were due to personal contacts, fostered by a common profession, travel, business relationships, military service, or other circumstances. Origen gives us a touching description of the zeal of these early missionaries:

> Christians do not neglect, as far as it lies within them, to take measures to disseminate their doctrine throughout the whole world. Some of them, accordingly, have made it their business to itinerate not only through cities, but even villages and country houses, that they might make converts to God. And no one would maintain that they did this for the sake of gain, when sometimes they would not accept even necessary sustenance.[2]

By the second half of the third century, these personal initiatives were increasingly coordinated and partly replaced by the local community. The bishop took the upper hand over the individual leaders, partly as a response to the erosive forces of the Gnostic heresy, and he became a director of the community's internal life and the driving force of its missionary activity.

---

* The *Didache* or *Teaching of the Twelve Apostles* is a treatise from the first or second century that deals with the Christian way of life. *Ed.*

The community was by now the principal evangelizer, to the point that Harnack,* not much of a sympathizer for the institution, said, "We may take it for granted that the mere existence and persistent activity of the individual Christian communities did more than anything else to bring about the extension of the Christian religion."[3]

Toward the end of the third century, the Christian faith had penetrated virtually every layer of society. By now it had its own literature in Greek and, to a lesser extent, in Latin; it had acquired a solid internal organization and was starting to construct larger buildings—a sign of the ever-increasing number of believers. The great persecution of Diocletian, apart from its many victims, did nothing but highlight the now unstoppable strength of the Christian faith. The last standoff between the empire and Christianity was proof of the latter's strength.

Emperor Constantine did nothing other than take note of the new equilibrium of powers. It was not he who imposed Christianity on the people, but the people who imposed Christianity on him. Lately, various writers have been promoting certain popular theories that due to personal reasons Constantine sought to transform an obscure Jewish sect into the religion of the empire through his edict of tolerance and the Council of Nicaea. But these suggestions are based on a total ignorance of what preceded those events.

2. The reasons for success

The successful growth of Christianity is a subject that has always fascinated historians. A message born among simple

---

* Adolf von Harnack (1851–1930), Lutheran theologian and historian noted for his rejection of traditional formulations of many dogmas. *Ed.*

people with no education or power, in an obscure and despised corner of the empire, expanded to the entire then-known world in less than three centuries. It overcame the refined culture of the Greeks and the imperial power of Rome! Among the various reasons given for Christianity's success, some have insisted on love and active charitable works. Some authors would make charity the single most powerful factor for its success, pointing to the fact that Emperor Julian the Apostate* provided paganism with similar works of charity in an attempt to compete with the success of Christianity.[4]

For his part, Harnack gives great importance to the Christian faith's ability to reconcile within itself the opposing trends and values of the different religions and cultures of its time. Christianity presented itself at the same time as the religion of the Spirit and of power, that is, it was accompanied by supernatural signs, gifts, and miracles, while at the same time being the religion of reason and the integral Logos—"the true philosophy," in the words of Saint Justin Martyr (ca. 100–165). Christian authors were "rationalists of the supernatural," notes Harnack, citing Saint Paul on the question of faith as "spiritual worship" (Rom 12:1).[5]

In this way, Christianity brought together in perfect equilibrium what the philosopher Friedrich Nietzsche defines as the Apollonian and Dionysian elements of the Greek religion: the Logos and the Pneuma, order and enthusiasm, balance and excess. This is what, at least in part, the Fathers of the Church intended by the theme of the "sober intoxication" of the Spirit. Harnack writes at the end of his monumental research:

---

* Julian the Apostate, Roman emperor from 361–363 was born to Christian parents but rejected Christianity. As emperor he attempted to restore pagan rituals and beliefs. *Ed.*

> From the very outset Christianity came forward with a spirit
> of universalism, by dint of which it laid hold of *the entire life
> of man* in all its functions, throughout its heights and depths,
> in all its feelings, thoughts, and actions. This guaranteed its
> triumph. In and with its universalism, it also declared that the
> Jesus whom it preached was the Logos. . . . Hence it was that
> those very powers of attraction, by means of which it was
> enabled at once to absorb and to subordinate the whole of
> Hellenism, had a new light thrown upon them. They appeared
> almost in the light of a necessary feature in that age. . . . And
> was not this religion bound to conquer?[6]

When reading this summary, one gets the impression that
Christianity's success was due to some specific set of factors.
Someone in particular has gone so far in searching for reasons
for its success as to determine precisely twenty causes in favor
of the faith and just as many against it, as if the final outcome
depended on the predominance of the former over the latter.

Here I would like to highlight the limits inherent in such
an historical approach, even if proposed by historians of faith,
such as those whom I have so far taken into account. The limit
of this historical method is that it gives more importance to the
subject rather than the object of the mission, more to the evan-
gelists and the conditions in which it took place than to its
content. I am highlighting this because it is also the limit and
danger inherent in many approaches in today's media when
speaking of the new evangelization. One simple thing is forgot-
ten: that Jesus himself previously explained the expansion of his
Gospel, and we must begin anew from that explanation each
time we prepare for a new missionary effort.

Let's consider two short parables of the Gospel—that of
the seed that grows at night and that of the mustard seed.

> [Jesus] also said, "The kingdom of God is as if someone
> would scatter seed on the ground, and would sleep and rise

night and day, and the seed would sprout and grow, he does not know how. The earth produces of itself, first the stalk, then the head, then the full grain in the head. But when the grain is ripe, at once he goes in with his sickle, because the harvest has come." (Mk 4:26–29)

This parable, in and of itself, tells us that the essential reason for the success of the Christian mission does not come from outside but from within. It is not the work of the sower, or even principally of the land, but of the seed. The seed cannot sow itself on its own, yet it sprouts automatically and of itself. After having sown the seed, the sower can even go to sleep, for the life of the seed no longer depends on him. When this seed is the seed that "falls into the earth and dies," that is, Jesus Christ, nothing can prevent it from bearing much fruit (see Jn 12:24). People can give all the explanations they want for this fruit, but those will always remain superficial and will never arrive at the essential.

The Apostle Paul perceived with clarity the priority of the Gospel message over the one who preaches it: "I planted, Apollos watered, but God gave the growth" (1 Cor 3:6). These words seem like a commentary on Jesus's parable. In fact, the apostle adds that the three matters are not given the same importance, "So neither the one who plants nor the one who waters is anything, but only God who gives the growth" (1 Cor 3:7). The same qualitative distance between the messenger and the message is present in another of the apostle's writings, "But we have this treasure in clay jars, so that it may be made clear that this extraordinary power belongs to God and does not come from us" (2 Cor 4:7). This is all summarized in the following proclamations, "For we do not proclaim ourselves; we proclaim Jesus Christ as Lord!" (2 Cor 4:5), and again, "We proclaim Christ crucified" (1 Cor 1:23).

Jesus gave a second parable based on the image of the seed that explains the success of the Christian mission. We need to take this into account today in the face of the immense task of re-evangelizing the secularized world.

> He also said, "With what can we compare the kingdom of God, or what parable will we use for it? It is like a mustard seed, which, when sown upon the ground, is the smallest of all the seeds on earth; yet when it is sown it grows up and becomes the greatest of all shrubs, and puts forth large branches, so that the birds of the air can make nests in its shade." (Mk 4:30–32)

Here Jesus teaches us that his Gospel and his own person are the smallest things that exist on the land, because nothing is smaller and weaker than a life that ends in death on a cross. Yet this small "mustard seed" is destined to become an immense tree, so as to receive in its branches all the birds that shall take refuge in it. All creation, absolutely all, will be able to find refuge there.

What a contrast to the historical revisionism mentioned above! Everything there seemed uncertain, random, and suspended between success or failure. Here, everything has already been decided and assured from the beginning! At the conclusion of the anointing at Bethany, Jesus said, "Truly I tell you, wherever this good news is proclaimed in the whole world, what she has done will be told in remembrance of her" (Mt 26:13). He spoke with the same calm awareness that one day his message would expand "to the ends of the earth." And it is certainly not a prophecy *post eventum* [after the event], since everything at that time was foreshadowing the opposite.

On this issue, Paul was able to foresee the future of the faith with great certainty. I am struck by this fact. The apostle preached at the Areopagus in Athens and witnessed, for all intents and purposes, a rejection of his message. He soon went to Corinth where he wrote the Letter to the Romans. In it, he claims to have been given the task of bringing about "the obedience of faith among all the Gentiles" (Rom 1:5–6). The failure had not in the least tarnished his trust in the message: "For I am not ashamed of the gospel," he cries out, "it is the power of God for salvation to everyone who has faith, to the Jew first and also to the Greek" (Rom 1:16).

Jesus says, "For each tree is known by its own fruit" (Lk 6:44). This applies to every tree, except the tree born of him—Christianity. (Actually, here he is speaking about humanity.) In Christianity, this tree alone is not recognized by its fruits but by its root. The fullness is not at the end (as in the Hegelian dialectic of becoming, according to which "truth is the whole"); rather, it is at the beginning.* No fruit, not even that represented by the greatest of saints, can add anything to the perfection of the model. In this sense the one who said, "Christianity is not perfectible" is right.[7]

3. Sow and then sleep

Regarding the origins of Christianity, historians seldom record, or at least attach little importance to, the unshakable certainty that Christians of that time (at least the best of them) had regarding the goodness and final victory of their cause. Saint Justin Martyr said to the Roman judge who sentenced him to death, "You can kill, but not hurt us."[8] In the end, this

---

* Georg Hegel (1770–1831), German philosopher who proposed a three-fold type of development: tension between a thesis and antithesis is resolved in a synthesis. *Ed.*

tranquil certainty assured them victory and convinced the political authorities of the futility of their efforts to suppress the Christian faith.

This is what we need most today: to awaken in Christians, at least in those who wish to dedicate themselves to the work of re-evangelization, the intimate certainty of the truth of what they proclaim. "The Church," Pope Paul VI once said, "needs to regain the eagerness, the zest, and the certainty of its truth."[9] We ourselves must be the first to believe in what we proclaim. We must truly believe it. We must be able to say with Paul, "But just as we have the same spirit of faith that is in accordance with scripture—'I believed, and so I spoke'—we also believe, and so we speak" (2 Cor 4:13). The success of the new evangelization will depend on the degree of faith that it successfully brings forth in the Church among the evangelizers themselves.

We must shake off every sense of powerlessness and resignation. Before us, it is true, we have a world that resists the proclamation of the Gospel. It is closed off within secularism, intoxicated by the success of technology and by opportunities that science offers. But was the world that the early Christians faced—that is, Hellenism with its wisdom and the Roman Empire with its power—any less confident in itself and less opposed to the Gospel?

The two parables of Jesus assign us a practical task: to sow. Sow with wide-open arms, "whether the time is favorable or unfavorable" (2 Tim 4:2). In the parable the one who goes out to sow does not care that some seeds may end up on the road and some among thorns. And to think that that sower is, in reality, Jesus himself! The reason is that, in this case, the sower cannot know in advance which ground will prove to be good and which will be as hard as asphalt or as suffocating as a weed. In the midst of it all is human freedom, which the evangelizer cannot predict and which God does not wish to go against.

How often do you find that, among people who have listened to a certain sermon or read some publication, the one who took it more seriously and changed his or her life is the person you least expected—the one who was there by chance perhaps, or even reluctantly? I myself could count dozens of cases in this regard.

Sow therefore, and then . . . go to sleep! That is, sow and do not linger to watch and measure the results. The sprouting and growth are not our business, but God's and the listener's. A great nineteenth-century English humorist, Jerome Klapka Jerome, once said that the best way to delay water from boiling in a pot is to linger over it and impatiently wait for it to boil. To do so is a source of uneasiness and impatience, things that Jesus does not like and never did while he was on earth. In the Gospel, Jesus never seems to be in a hurry. "So do not worry about tomorrow, for tomorrow will bring worries of its own. Today's trouble is enough for today" (Mt 6:34). The poet Charles Péguy, a believer, placed these words in the mouth of God:

"I am told that there are men," says God,
"Who work well and sleep badly.
Who do not sleep. Who lack confidence in me.
It would be better
If they did not work but slept, because laziness
Is not a greater sin than uneasiness . . .
I am not speaking," says God, "of those men
Who do not work and do not sleep.
Those are sinners, you see . . .
I am speaking of those who work and do not sleep . . .
I pity them. I'm irritated with them. Just a little. They do not
　　trust me . . .

They manage their affairs well during the day.
But they do not want to entrust their governance to me during
    the night . . .
The one who does not sleep is unfaithful to Hope. . . ."10

This is a poetic way of speaking, but it contains great evangelical wisdom for those who know how to listen to it.

After sowing we can do one thing—water the sown seed with prayer. For this reason, let us conclude this first reflection with the liturgical prayer of the Mass for the Evangelization of Peoples:

O God, you want all people to be saved
and to come to the knowledge of the truth;
look at how great is your harvest and send your workers,
so that the Gospel may be proclaimed to every creature
and your people, gathered together by the word of life
and shaped by the power of the sacraments,
proceed in the way of salvation and love.
Through Christ our Lord. Amen.

CHAPTER 2

There Is No Longer Greek or Jew, Barbarian or Scythian

The new wave of evangelization
after the invasions of
the Roman Empire

Now let us turn to the second great wave of evangelization in the history of the Church—the one that followed the collapse of the Roman Empire and the reshuffling of populations caused by the invasions. We do so always with the practical purpose of seeing what we can learn from it today. Given the breadth of the historical period we are about to examine, I can only offer a simple reconstruction from a broad perspective.

1. A momentous decision

At the end of the Roman Empire in 476, Europe had long since had a new face. Instead of one empire, there were many so-called Roman-barbarian kingdoms. Broadly speaking, this was the situation, starting from the north: the Angles and the Saxons were in the former Roman province of Britannia (Britain); the Franks were in the ancient province of Gallia (Gaul); the Frisians and the Alemanni were east of the Rhine; the Visigoths were in the Iberian Peninsula; the Ostrogoths and later the Lombards were in Italy; the Vandals were in North Africa; and in the East, the Byzantine Empire was still resisting.

A momentous decision faced the Church: What attitude should it adopt regarding this new situation? The decision that opened the Church to the future was not arrived at immediately or without difficulties. The Church repeated, in part, what had happened much earlier when it separated from Judaism and accepted Gentiles within the Church. The general bewilderment of the Christians reached its peak in 410 when Alaric, king of the Goths, sacked Rome. It was thought that the end of the world had arrived, as the world was then identified with the Roman world and the Roman world with Christianity. Saint

Jerome, the most representative voice of this general confusion, wrote, "Who would believe that Rome, built up by the conquest of the whole world, had collapsed?"[1]

From an intellectual point of view, Saint Augustine contributed the most toward ferrying the faith into the new world with his work *De civitate Dei* [*The City of God*]. In his vision, which marked the beginning of the philosophy of history, he distinguished the city of God from the earthly city, identified at times (interjecting his own thought a bit) with the city of Satan. By earthly city, he meant every political order, including that of Rome. So, the fall of Rome was not the end of *the* world, but only the end of *a* world!

In practice, the Roman pontiff played a key role in opening the faith to the new reality and coordinating its initiatives. Saint Leo the Great had a clear awareness that Christian Rome would survive pagan Rome, and, as a matter of fact, Rome "attain[ed] a wider sway by the worship of God than by earthly government."[2]

Gradually, the attitude of Christians toward outside peoples changed. From being thought of as inferior beings, incapable of civilization, they began to be considered as potential future brothers and sisters in the faith. From a permanent threat, the pagan world began to appear to the Christians as a new and vast mission field. Paul had proclaimed the abolition in Christ of the distinctions of race, religion, culture, and social class with these words: "there is no longer Greek and Jew, circumcised and uncircumcised, barbarian, Scythian, slave and free; but Christ is all and in all!" (Col 3:11). But how much effort still remained to transform this revolution into practice! And not only in that era!

2. The re-evangelization of Europe

Confronted with the Germanic and other peoples, the Church found itself fighting two battles. The first was against the Arian heresy.* Many tribes, especially the Goths, had come into contact with Christianity in the East before entering the heart of the empire as conquerors. They had embraced Christianity in its Arian version as it was practiced there, partly due to the efforts of the Arian bishop Ulfilas (311–383), who translated the Bible into the Gothic language. The Goths brought with them this heretical version of Christianity when they went to the western territories.

Arianism, however, did not have a unified organization, culture, or theology comparable to that of Catholicism. During the sixth century, one after the other, the tribal kingdoms abandoned Arianism to adhere to the Catholic faith. This was due to the work of some great bishops and Catholic writers, as well as various political moves. In 589 the Council of Toledo, led by Leander of Seville, marked a decisive moment—the end of Arianism in Visigothic Spain and, practically speaking, the entire West.

The battle against Arianism, however, was not something new; it had begun as far back as 325. At the twilight of the Roman Empire, the Church accomplished the truly new feat of evangelizing the pagans. This happened in two areas: with the nations of the ancient empire and with those who had recently appeared on the scene. In the territories of the ancient empire, its provinces, and Italy, the Church had until then planted itself almost exclusively in the cities. It now extended its presence in the countryside and in villages. The term "pagan"

---

* The Arian heresy denied the divinity of Christ, claiming he was inferior to God the Father. The Council of Nicaea refuted this in 325. *Ed.*

comes, in fact, from the Latin word *pagus*, which means "village." It derived its present meaning from the fact that evangelization efforts in the countryside generally occurred much later than those in cities.

It would certainly be interesting to follow this line of evangelization, which led to the birth and development of the system of parishes as subdivisions of the diocese. But for my present purpose, I must limit myself to the other area of evangelization. This was to bring the Gospel to the peoples settled in the insular and central part of Europe, that is, today's England, Holland, France, and Germany.

A decisive moment in this effort was the conversion of the Merovingian king, Clovis, who was baptized on Christmas Eve of 498 or 499 by the bishop of Rheims, Saint Remigius.* Therefore, according to the custom of the time, he determined not just the religious future of the Frankish people, but also that of other nations on both sides of the Rhine River whom he conquered. As he baptized Clovis, Bishop Remigius said the famous words, *"Mitis depone colla, Sigamber; adora quod incendisti, incende quod adorasti"* ("Gently bend your neck, Sigamber; worship what you burned; burn what you worshipped").3 The nation of France owes its title as "eldest daughter of the Church" to this event.

Thanks to the work of Saints Cyril and Methodius, the Christianization of the continent was completed by the ninth century with the conversion of the Slavic nations. These peoples had occupied the territories in Eastern Europe that had been vacated by previous waves of western migration.

---

* The date of Clovis's baptism is uncertain. The traditional date, April 13, 496, is debated by historians. *Ed.*

The conversion of the pagan peoples presented a new condition with respect to the Greco-Roman world. There, Christianity encountered a cultured and organized society that had ordinances, laws, and common languages. It had, in short, a culture in which to dialogue and contend with people. With regard to the other peoples, Christianity was dealing with the work of civilization in addition to evangelization; the evangelizers had to teach people to read and write, besides catechizing them in Christian doctrine. Inculturation presented itself there under an entirely new form.

3. The monastic era

This enormous work of evangelization, which I can only highlight here, was carried out with the participation of all members of the Church, in the first place, the popes.* Their direct initiative led to the evangelization of the Angles, and they played an active part in the evangelization of Germany (through the work of Saint Boniface) and the Slavic nations (through the work of Saints Cyril and Methodius). Next, bishops and pastors played a role in these efforts as they gradually formed local stable communities. Women played a silent but decisive role, especially the wives of some of the kings who had great conversions: Saint Clotilde in the case of Clovis; Saint Theodelinda for the Lombard King Authari; and the Catholic wife of King Edwin, who introduced Christianity in northern England.

But the monks were undoubtedly the protagonists who took leading roles in the re-evangelization of Europe after the

---

* The Popes referred to here are Gregory I the Great (the Angles), Gregory II (the Germans), and Nicholas I and Adrian II (the Slavs). *Ed.*

invasions. In the West, monasticism began in the fourth century and quickly expanded in two periods and from two different directions. The first wave began in southern and central Gaul, especially at Lérins (410) and Auxerre (418). Thanks to Saint Patrick, who had received formation in those two centers, the Gospel reached Ireland and influenced its entire religious landscape. From there it passed to Scotland with Saint Columba, founder of Iona (521–597), and to northern England with Saint Cuthbert of Lindisfarne (635–687). Thus, Christianity and monasticism were established in these places with a certain Celtic makeup.

The second monastic wave originated in Italy with Saint Benedict (ca. 480–547). This form, more Roman, would eventually gain the upper hand and unify the other styles of Western monasticism. The monk Augustine and his companions belonged to this wave, and Pope Gregory the Great sent them to Britain, where they evangelized southern England. They brought a Roman form of Christianity, which ended up prevailing over the Celtic form and harmonized the British Isles with the rest of Christianity (for example, regarding the date of Easter).

From the fifth through the eighth centuries, Europe would literally become covered in monasteries. Many of these played a primary role in the formation of the continent, not only in terms of faith, but also regarding art, culture, and agriculture. For this reason, Saint Benedict was proclaimed the patron saint of Europe, and in 2005 Cardinal Ratzinger, a few days before his election to the papacy, chose Mount Subiaco for his lecture on the Christian roots of Europe.

The great figures of evangelizing monks on the continent belonged almost entirely to the first of the two currents mentioned above—the one that would return to the continent from

Ireland and England. The two most representative monks were Saint Columbanus (ca. 543–615) and Saint Boniface (ca. 672–754). Columbanus, departing from Luxeuil, evangelized many regions in northern Gaul and among the southern Germanic tribes, going all the way down to Bobbio, Italy. Boniface, considered the evangelizer of Germany, extended his missionary activity from Fulda, Germany, to Friesland, in today's Netherlands. Reading about their lives gives the impression that they were reliving the missionary adventures of the Apostle Paul. They had the same eagerness to take the Gospel to every creature, the same courage to face all sorts of dangers and hardships and, for Saint Boniface and many others, the same ultimate fate of martyrdom.

The weaknesses of this evangelization outreach have been noted, and a comparison with Saint Paul highlights the most relevant one. As part of his evangelization efforts, the apostle always carefully looked after the foundation of a church to assure its continuity and development. Due to scarce resources and the difficulty of moving about in a developing society, these pioneering monks were often not able to assure the stability of their work.

Regarding the previously-mentioned admonition of Saint Remigius to Clovis, the pagan peoples tended to put into practice only one part of it: they worshipped what they had burned, but they did not burn what they had worshipped, and much of their idolatrous and pagan past remained to rear its head at the first opportunity. It happened as with certain roads through a forest. Since they are not properly maintained, or seldom used, the roads are soon taken over by the surrounding thick forest. The most lasting work of these great evangelizers was the foundation of a network of monasteries. With Saint Augustine in England and Saint Boniface in Germany, the erection of dioceses and the celebration of synods would ensure that their evangelization efforts would continue in longer-lasting and more solid ways.

4. Mission and contemplation

Now I would like to draw some lessons for today from this historical overview. First, we notice a certain analogy between the era we just revisited and our current situation. At that time, population movement was from east to west; today, it is from south to north. Through its teaching, the Church has also taken a stand in this regard, by being open to the new situation and welcoming the new peoples.

The difference today, however, is that immigrants to Europe and other northern countries are not pagans or Christian heretics; instead, they already possess a well-established religion, to which they are very attached. So the new key word today is dialogue, which is not opposed to evangelization, but rather determines its style. Saint John Paul II expressed himself clearly on the subject of the permanent validity of the missionary mandate:

> Interreligious dialogue is a part of the Church's evangelizing mission. Understood as a method and means of mutual knowledge and enrichment, dialogue is not in opposition to the mission *ad gentes*; indeed, it has special links with that mission and is one of its expressions [. . .]. In the light of the economy of salvation, the Church sees no conflict between proclaiming Christ and engaging in interreligious dialogue. Instead, she feels the need to link the two in the context of her mission *ad gentes*. These two elements must maintain both their intimate connection and their distinctiveness; therefore they should not be confused, manipulated or regarded as identical, as though they were interchangeable.[4]

What happened in Europe after the invasions shows us, above all, the importance of the contemplative life, especially in view of evangelization. With respect to this, the Second Vatican Council says:

> Worthy of special mention are the various projects for caus-
> ing the contemplative life to take root. There are those who in
> such an attempt have kept the essential element of a monas-
> tic institution, and are bent on implanting the rich tradition
> of their order; there are others again who are returning to the
> simpler forms of ancient monasticism. But all are studiously
> looking for a genuine adaptation to local conditions. Since
> the contemplative life belongs to the fullness of the Church's
> presence, let it be put into effect everywhere.[5]

This invitation to seek new forms of monasticism in view of evangelization, while still being inspired by ancient monasticism, has not gone unheeded. One of the ways in which this wish has been fulfilled is through the Monastic Fraternities of Jerusalem, whose members are known as "monks and nuns of the city." Their founder, Father Pierre-Marie Delfieux, spent two years in the Sahara Desert possessing only the Eucharist and the Bible. He realized that the true desert today is in large secularized cities. Begun in Paris on the feast of All Saints Day (November 1) in 1975, these fraternities are now present in several major European cities, including Rome, where they have established themselves at the Church of Santissima Trinità dei Monti. Their charism is to evangelize through the beauty of art and liturgy. Their habit, their simple and austere lifestyle, and the way they combine work and prayer are tradi-tionally monastic. Novel elements, however, include their position in the center of the city (usually in ancient churches of great artistic value) and the collaboration between monks and nuns, who share liturgical prayer in common while remaining completely independent from one another in terms of living space and obedience. These places have led to many profound conversions and the return of quite a few nominal Christians to the faith.

The monastery of Bose in Italy, although of a different kind, is part of these flowering new monastic forms.* Another example of the contemplative life directly engaged in evangelization is the ecumenical community and monastery of Taizé in France.

On November 1, 1982, in Avila, while welcoming many representatives of women's contemplative orders, John Paul II envisaged the possibility of their having a more direct commitment in the work of evangelization. He said to the women religious:

> Your monasteries are communities of prayer amid Christian communities, which you help and nourish, and to which you give hope. They are consecrated places and can also be centers of Christian welcome for those people, especially the young, who are often searching for a simpler and more transparent life in contrast to what a consumer society offers them.[6]

His appeal was not ignored and has been realized in many fresh initiatives to establish women's contemplative communities open to evangelization. These new forms of religious life have not replaced traditional monastic forms, many of which radiate spirituality and are also centers of evangelization; rather, they complement and enrich them.

It is not enough that some in the Church dedicate themselves to contemplation while others are missionaries. Instead, a synthesis of the two should occur in the life of every missionary.

---

* The ecumenical Monastic Community of Bose was established in 1965 by the Catholic layman Enzo Bianchi. *Ed.*

It is not enough, in other words, to pray "for" the missionaries; instead, there should be the prayer "of" the missionaries. The great monks who re-evangelized Europe after the invasions were men who had emerged out of the silence of their contemplation, to which they returned as soon as circumstances permitted. In fact, in their heart they never entirely left the monastery. They had already put into practice the guidance that Francis of Assisi gave to his brothers before sending them out on the roads of the world: "Wherever we are, wherever we go, we bring our cell with us. Our brother body is our cell and our soul is the hermit living in that cell in order to pray to God and meditate."[7]

On this topic, we have a much more authoritative example than that of the saints. The daily life of Jesus was a wonderful blend of prayer and preaching. He not only prayed before preaching, but he also prayed to know what to preach, in order to draw from prayer the things to announce to the world. "What I speak," he said, "I speak just as the Father has told me" (Jn 12:50). Jesus drew from prayer the authority that so marked his speech.

The effort of the new evangelization faces two dangers: one is inertia, laziness, not doing anything and letting others do all the work; the other is launching into many busy but ultimately empty, human activities. Little by little, this results in losing contact with the source of the Word and its strength. Some have asked how we can sit quietly at prayer while so many needs demand our presence? How can we sit still while the house is burning down? They have a valid point. But let's imagine what would happen to a unit of firefighters who rushed to put out a fire, but once at the scene, realized they did not have a single drop of water in their tanks. This is exactly how we are when we rush to preach without praying first.

Prayer is essential for evangelization because Christian preaching is not primarily the communication of a doctrine but of a way of being. The one who prays without speaking does more evangelization than the one who speaks without praying.

5. Mary, Star of Evangelization

Let us conclude this chapter with a reflection on the Virgin. Once during an ecumenical dialogue, a Protestant brother asked me (in a non-polemical way, for he truly wanted to understand), "Why do you Catholics say that Mary is 'the star of evangelization'? What did Mary do to justify such a title?" It was an opportunity for me to reflect on this, and it didn't take long to discover the profound answer. Mary is the star of evangelization because she brought the Word not to one particular nation or race but to the whole world!

And this is not the only reason. She carried the Word in her womb, not on her mouth. Even physically she was full of Christ, and she radiated him by her mere presence. She emitted Jesus from her eyes, from her face, from her whole person. A person who is fragrant with a pleasant perfume does not need to say that; simply being nearby is enough to notice. Mary was full of the fragrance of Christ, especially while she was carrying Jesus in her womb.

It can be said that Mary was the first cloistered woman in the Church. After Pentecost, it appears as if she entered a monastic enclosure. Through the letters of the apostles, we come to know of countless figures (including many women) within the early Christian community. A certain Mary is mentioned (see Rom 16:6), but she is not the Mother of Jesus. Nothing is said of Mary, the Mother of Jesus, as if she has disappeared in the deepest silence. But what did it mean for John to have her near him while he wrote his Gospel? And what could it mean for us to keep her near us while we proclaim the same Gospel? "John is the first fruit of the [four] Gospels. No one can understand its meaning unless he has lain on Jesus's breast and received from him Mary, as his own mother also."[8]

Mary inaugurated that second soul, or vocation, within the Church—that is, the hidden and prayerful soul, alongside the apostolic or active soul. This is expressed wonderfully by a traditional icon of the Ascension. Mary is standing with her arms open in a prayerful posture. Around her, the apostles—with a foot or a hand raised in motion—represent the active Church that goes out on mission, speaking and acting. Mary is motionless under Jesus in the exact spot from which he ascended, as if to keep alive his memory and the expectation of his return.

Let us conclude by listening to the final words of *Evangelii Nuntiandi* by Pope Paul VI. This is the first time in papal documents that the title "Star of Evangelization" is used for Mary:

> On the morning of Pentecost she watched over with her prayer the beginning of evangelization prompted by the Holy Spirit: may she be the Star of the Evangelization ever renewed that the Church, docile to her Lord's command, must promote and accomplish, especially in these times, which are difficult but full of hope![9]

CHAPTER 3

To the Ends of the Earth

The first evangelization
of the Americas

1. The Christian faith crosses the ocean

This chapter will deal with the third largest wave of evangelization in the history of the Church—the one that followed the discovery of the New World. Let us briefly call to mind how this missionary endeavor unfolded. But first an observation: Christian Europe exported its divisions, as well as its faith, to the new continent. At the end of the great missionary wave, the American continent would replicate exactly the same situation as in Europe: a Catholic majority in the South with a corresponding Protestant majority in the North. Here we will only deal with the evangelization of Latin America, since it took place first, immediately after the discovery of the New World.

After Christopher Columbus returned from his voyage in 1492 with reports of the existence of new lands (which he at first believed were part of India), two inseparably linked decisions were made in Catholic Spain. The first was to bring the new people into the Christian faith, and the second was to extend Spain's political sovereignty over them. To this end, a decision was obtained from Pope Alexander VI that recognized the right of Spain to rule over all the lands that were discovered three hundred miles west of the Azores, and to Portugal all those lands east of that line. Afterward, this line was shifted in favor of Portugal in order to legitimize its possession of Brazil.*
In this way, the future face of the Latin American continent was outlined, as well as its languages.

While penetrating into a particular area, the Spanish troops would issue a proclamation (*requerimiento*) that ordered the inhabitants both to embrace Christianity and to recognize the sovereignty of the king of Spain.[1] Only a few great souls had

---

* This refers to the papal decree *Inter Caetera* of May 4, 1493. *Ed.*

the courage to speak out against the abuses of the conquistadors and to defend the rights of the natives, for example, the two Dominicans—Antonio de Montesinos and Bartolomé de Las Casas. Partly due to the weaknesses and divisions of its local kingdoms, in little more than fifty years the continent was under Spanish and Portuguese dominion and was at least nominally Christian.

Recent historians have tended to soften the negative judgments given in the past regarding this time of missionary activity. First, they point out that, unlike what would take place regarding the native tribes in North America, in Latin America, despite their being decimated, the majority of the native peoples survived with their own language in their own territory. They were also later allowed to reclaim and recover their own identity and independence.

We must also consider how the theological formation of the missionaries influenced their attitudes. These missionaries were accustomed to taking literally and rigidly applying the axiom *extra Ecclesiam nulla salus* ("outside the Church there is no salvation"). Therefore, they were convinced that they needed to baptize as many people in the shortest time possible in order to ensure their eternal salvation.

It is worth considering this axiom for a moment, since it was such a weighty factor in their evangelization. It was formulated in the third century by Origen and, above all, by Saint Cyprian. At first, it did not deal with the salvation of non-Christians, but only that of Christians. It was directed exclusively at the heretics and schismatics of the time, and it reminded them that they were guilty of grave sin in breaking ecclesial communion. Therefore, they excluded themselves from salvation. Hence, it was directed at those who were leaving the Church, not at those who did not enter it. Only later, when Christianity had become the state religion, did the axiom begin to be applied to pagans and Jews. At that point, it was commonly believed (even though incorrectly) that the message was known by all people, and therefore to reject it meant to make oneself guilty and deserving of condemnation.

Precisely in the years after the discovery of the New World, those geographical boundaries were broken dramatically. The discovery of entire races and peoples who lived outside of any contact with the Church forced a revision of such a rigid interpretation of the axiom. The Dominican theologians of Salamanca (and later some Jesuits) began to adopt a critical viewpoint. They acknowledged it was possible to be outside the Church without necessarily being guilty and, therefore, excluded from salvation. Not only that, but due to the manner and inadequate methods with which the Gospel was announced to the native peoples, some theologians, for the first time, raised the question as to whether or not they could consider culpable all those who did not adhere to the Christian announcement, even if they had heard it.[2]

2. The friars as protagonists

This is certainly not the place to make an historical judgment on the initial evangelization of Latin America. On the occasion of the fifth centenary of the discovery of the Americas, an international symposium of historians was held in Rome to consider this subject. In his address to the participants, John Paul II stated: "Certainly in this evangelization, as in any human endeavor, there were successes and mistakes, lights and shadows, but more lights than shadows to judge by the fruits we find there five hundred years later: a living and dynamic Church that today represents a significant portion of the universal Church."[3]

On the same occasion, some on the opposite spectrum spoke of a need for "deculturation" and "de-evangelization." They seemed to prefer that the evangelization of the continent had never taken place at all, rather than having taken place in the way we know. While respecting the love for the native peoples that moved these authors, I believe that such an opinion should be vigorously refuted. To a world without sin, but also without Jesus Christ, theology has always preferred a world with sin, but with Jesus Christ.* "O happy fault," exclaims the Paschal Liturgy in the *Exultet*, "that earned so great, so glorious a Redeemer." Should we not say the same of the evangelization of both Americas, South and North? To a continent without the "mistakes and shadows" that accompanied its evangelization, but also without Christ, who would not prefer a continent with such shadows, but also with Christ? What Christian, on the right or the left, could say otherwise without betraying their faith for that very reason?

I read somewhere a statement that I fully agree with: "The greatest thing that happened in 1492 was not that Christopher Columbus discovered America, but that America discovered Jesus Christ." True, he was not the integral Christ of the Gospel in which freedom is the prerequisite of the faith, but who can claim to be the bearer of a Christ free of any historical conditioning? Do not those who propose a revolutionary Christ —protester of institutions and directly involved even in the political struggle—perhaps forget something else of Christ, for

---

* The author is referring to the idea that the Incarnation occurred only because of human sin. Saint Thomas Aquinas held this position (*Summa Theol.* III, q. 1, a. 3), but other theologians have held that God would have brought about the Incarnation even if humanity had not sinned. *Ed.*

example, his statement, "my kingdom is not from this world" (Jn 18:36)?

In the first wave of evangelization the protagonists were the bishops, and in the second wave they were the monks. In this third wave, the undisputed leading participants were the friars, that is, the religious mendicant orders. The Franciscans, Dominicans, and Augustinians came first, and the Jesuits came later. Church historians recognize that in Latin America, "the members of religious orders determined the history of the missions and of the churches."[4]

In this regard, the previously-mentioned judgment of John Paul II should be noted here: there are "more lights than shadows." It would be dishonest to underestimate the personal sacrifices and heroic deeds of many of these missionaries. While many conquistadors were motivated by a spirit of adventure and thirst for gain, what could these friars and priests hope for after having left their homeland and religious communities? They did not go to take but to give. They wanted to conquer souls for Christ, not produce subjects for the king of Spain, even if they often shared the same patriotic zeal as their fellow countrymen. When one reads stories related to the evangelization of a particular territory, one sees readily how unjust and far from reality it is to make unfounded generalizations. In fact, once while I was in Guatemala, I read an account on the beginning of the mission there and in surrounding regions. These are stories of sacrifice and untold misfortunes. Out of a group of twenty Dominicans who left for the New World bound for the Philippines, eighteen died during the trip.

In 1974 a synod was held on the topic of "Evangelization in the Modern World." In a note, written in his own hand in the margin of the final document, Pope Paul VI wrote:

Has enough been said about the religious? Should a word about the original, enterprising, and generous character of the evangelization of the men and women religious be said? Their missionary activity must depend on the hierarchy and must be coordinated with the pastoral plan which the latter adopts. But the immense contribution that these religious brought and continue to bring to evangelization, often risking their health and their very lives, should be praised.

This recognition fully applies to those friars who played leading roles in the evangelization of Latin America. This is especially so when we think of some of their accomplishments, such as the Jesuits' famous "Reductions" in Paraguay. These were villages where the indigenous Christians were safe from the abuses of civil authorities and could be catechized in the faith. But they were also places where they could develop and make the most of their human talents.

3. Current problems

As we have done previously, let us now fast-forward to the present in order to see what the history of the missionary experience of the Church (which we have briefly reviewed) can tell us today. The social and religious conditions of the continent have changed so profoundly that, rather than insist on what we can learn or unlearn from that time, it would be more useful to reflect on the task of today's evangelization in Latin America.

Since we have a great deal of reflection and documents on this subject from papal teaching, the Latin America Episcopal Conference (CELAM), and the local churches, it would be presumptuous of me to think that I could add anything new. Nonetheless, I can share some reflections as a result of my experience in the field, as I have had the opportunity to preach retreats to various episcopal conferences, the clergy, and the people of nearly every Latin American country—some of them more than once. Besides, the problems that arise regarding this issue in Latin America are not so different from those of the rest of the Church.

One reflection deals with the need to overcome an excessive polarization that exists practically everywhere in the Church, but is particularly acute in Latin America, especially in past years. This is the polarization between the active soul and the contemplative soul, between the Church of social commitment to the poor and the Church that proclaims the faith. Before such differences, we are instinctively tempted to take sides and praise one position while despising the other. The doctrine of charisms, however, should save us from that struggle. One of the gifts of the Catholic Church is that it is *catholic*, that is, it is open to receiving diverse gifts from the same Spirit.

The history of religious orders demonstrates this, as they internalize different and sometimes opposing demands: to engage the world and to retreat from the world; apostolic work aimed at the learned, such as the Jesuits perform, and apostolic work among the common people, such as the Capuchins perform. The Church has room for the one as well as the other. Moreover, we need each other, since no individual can fulfill all the demands of the entire Gospel and represent Christ in all aspects of his life. Each person should, therefore, rejoice that others can do what he or she cannot: those dedicated to the spiritual life and the proclamation of the Word should rejoice that others have committed themselves to social justice and human advancement, and vice versa. Saint Paul's admonition is always valid, "Let us therefore no longer pass judgment on one another" (Rom 14:13).

A second observation concerns the problem of Catholics leaving the Church for other Christian denominations. First, we must remember that we cannot indiscriminately qualify these various denominations as "sects." With some of them, including the Pentecostals, the Catholic Church has maintained an official ecumenical dialogue for years, something it would not do if it considered them to be simply sects.

The promotion of this dialogue, especially at the local level, is the best way to improve the situation, isolate the more aggressive sects, and discourage proselytism. A few years ago in Buenos Aires, an ecumenical meeting was held to pray together and share the Word. The Catholic archbishop,* Cardinal Bergoglio, participated together with the leaders of other churches; in fact, seven thousand people were present. It is clearly evident that the possibility exists for a new relationship among Christians, one far more constructive for faith and evangelization.

In one of his documents, John Paul II affirmed that the spread of sects should force us to ask ourselves why they are increasing and, thus, what is lacking in our own pastoral praxis. Based on my own experience—and not just in the countries of Latin America—I believe the following: what attracts believers outside the Church is certainly not that they offer alternative forms of popular piety (which, in fact, most of the other churches and sects reject and fight against); rather, they incisively, even if perhaps partially, proclaim God's grace. They offer people the chance to experience Jesus as their personal Lord and Savior, to belong to a group that will take care of their personal needs, and to have people pray over them during sickness when medicine can no longer do anything.

---

* Though the author doesn't give the date, this probably refers to Cardinal Jorge Bergoglio, now Pope Francis. *Ed.*

If, on the one hand, we can rejoice that these people have found Christ and have been converted, then, on the other, it is sad to know that in order to do so, they felt the need to leave their own Church. In the majority of the churches where these brothers and sisters end up, everything revolves around their initial conversion and acceptance of Jesus as Lord. In the Catholic Church, thanks to the sacraments, Church teaching, and a rich spirituality, we have the advantage of not stopping at the beginning stage, but reaching the fullness and perfection of the Christian life. The saints are proof of this. But it is important that a personal and free preliminary step is taken, and it is here that the evangelical communities and Pentecostal churches challenge us.

In this respect, the charismatic renewal has proved to be more than ever, according to the words of Pope Paul VI, "a chance for the Church."5 In Latin America, the Church's pastors are realizing that the charismatic renewal is not (as some initially believed) part of the problem of the exodus of Catholics from the Church, but is instead part of the solution. Statistics will never tell us how many people have remained faithful to the Church because of this movement, finding within it precisely what others sought elsewhere. The many communities born from within the charismatic renewal, despite its limitations and sometimes excesses (present in every human enterprise), are at the forefront of service to the Church and evangelization.

4. The role of religious in the new evangelization

I said that I did not want to dwell on the evangelization of the past. We should, however, consider one aspect of it: the importance of long-established religious orders. Saint John Paul II dedicated his apostolic letter to them on the occasion of the fifth centenary of the initial evangelization of the continent, titled in the original Spanish, *Los caminos del Evangelio.* The last part of the letter, in fact, deals with "religious in the new evangelization." The Pope wrote:

> The religious, who were the first evangelists—and who have contributed in such a relevant manner to keep the faith alive in the continent—cannot be skipped by this ecclesial convocation on the new evangelization. The different charisms of consecrated life renew the message of Jesus, present and real in every time and place.[6]

The religious orders of that time were able to exercise quite a vast missionary enterprise due to their life in community, central government, and formation houses of the highest quality. But what is left today of their original energy? Speaking from the inside of one of these very old orders, I can venture to express myself with a certain freedom. The rapid decline in vocations in the Western countries is causing a dangerous situation. The risk is that we now spend most of our energy in meeting the internal needs of our religious communities (formation of the young, maintenance of the religious houses and works, and so on), without much energy left for service to the wider Church. Hence, we risk turning in on ourselves. In Europe, the traditional religious orders have been forced to merge numerous provinces into one and to painfully close one house after another.

Secularization is, of course, one of the reasons for the decline in vocations, but not the only one. A number of recently founded religious communities are attracting scores of young people. In the letter already quoted, John Paul II exhorted the men and women religious of Latin America to "evangelize from a profound experience of God." And that, I believe, is the point: "a profound experience of God." That is what attracts vocations and will pave the way for a powerful new wave of evangelization. The old adage, *"Nemo dat quod non habet"* ("No one can give what he does not have"), is valid today more than ever in this regard.

The provincial minister of the Capuchin friars of the Marches region in Italy (who is also my own superior) wrote a letter to all the friars in our province. In it, he presents a challenge which I think is good for all traditional religious communities to hear:

> You who read these sentences must imagine that you are "the Holy Spirit." Yes, you understood me properly: not only to be "filled with the Holy Spirit" thanks to the sacraments you have received, but truly "to be" the Holy Spirit—the Third Person of the Holy Trinity. And, in this guise, consider that you have the power to call and send a young man in such a way that it would help him to walk toward the perfection of charity—religious life, to be explicit. Would you have the courage to send him to your friary with the certainty and assurance that your friary will be the place to help him earnestly reach the perfection of charity in the concreteness of everyday life? In short: if a young man were to come and live in your friary for a few days or months, to share in the life of prayer and fraternal life, and participate in your apostolates . . . would he fall in love with our life?

The Franciscan and Dominican mendicant orders were born at the beginning of the thirteenth century. Even the existing monastic orders benefited from them because the mendicants called them to greater poverty and a more evangelical life, all the while remaining faithful to their own charisms. Should not we, the traditional orders of today, do the same toward the new forms of consecrated life now springing up within the Church?

The grace of these new situations is multifaceted but has a common denominator: the Holy Spirit—the "new Pentecost."

After the Second Vatican Council, almost all the preexisting religious orders reviewed and updated their constitutions. Yet, in 1981, John Paul II admonished: "The whole work of renewal of the Church, so providentially set forth and initiated by the Second Vatican Council . . . can be carried out only in the Holy Spirit, that is to say, with the aid of his light and his power."[7] "The Holy Spirit," said Saint Bonaventure, goes "where he is loved, where he is invited, where he is awaited."[8] We must open our communities to the breath of the Spirit, who renews prayer, life in community, love for Christ, and, along with this, missionary zeal. We must certainly look back to our origins and founders, but also look ahead.

While observing the situation of the ancient orders in the Western world, the question that Ezekiel heard before the vastness of dry bones arises, "Can these bones live?" (see Ez 37:1–14). The dry bones mentioned in the text are not of the dead but of the living; they are the people of Israel in exile who are saying, "Our bones are dried up, and our hope is lost; we are cut off completely." These same feelings sometimes also emerge in us—those of us who belong to religious orders of ancient date.

We know the answer, full of hope, that God gives to that question: "I will cause breath to enter you, and you shall live . . . I will bring you back to the land of Israel. And you shall know that I am the LORD . . . I, the LORD, have spoken and will act" (Ez 37:5, 12, 14). We must believe and hope that what was said at the end of the prophecy will come true for us and for the whole Church, "the breath came into them, and they lived, and stood on their feet, a vast multitude" (Ez 37:10).

In conclusion, let us return to the evangelization of the American continent. It is of great symbolic significance that in 1531—right at the beginning—on Tepeyac hill, just north of

Mexico City, the image of the Virgin was imprinted on the *tilma* (the cloak of Saint Juan Diego) as *La Morenita,* that is, she had the features of a humble *mestizo,* a girl of mixed heritage. Could it not be said in any more suggestive manner how the Church in Latin America is called to be . . . and should be? That is, indigenous to the indigenous peoples, everything to everyone?

Much discussion has taken place about the historicity of the facts that lie at the origin of the devotion to the Virgin of Guadalupe. Yet, we need to be clear on what is meant by historic fact. There are many facts that indeed happened and are *historical* but are not *historic,* because "historic" in its truest sense is not just any event that took place or merely happened, but only that which had a bearing on something in the life of a people, created something new, and left a mark in history. And what a mark the devotion to the Virgin of Guadalupe left on the religious history of the people of Mexico and Latin America!

CHAPTER 4

Starting from the Beginning

The wave of evangelization
in action

41

1. A new recipient of the proclamation

So far, I have tried to reconstruct the three great waves of evangelization in the history of the Church. One could certainly recall other great missionary enterprises: the one to the East begun by Saint Francis Xavier in the sixteenth century and the one to the African continent in the nineteenth century by Daniel Comboni, Cardinal Guglielmo Massaia, and so many others. Nevertheless, I hope the reason for my choice has emerged from the reflections carried out. What changes and distinguishes the various waves of evangelization mentioned is not the object of the announcement—"the faith that was once for all entrusted to the saints," as the Letter of Jude (v. 3) calls it—but its respective recipients: the Greco-Roman world, the barbarian world, and the New World, namely, the American continents.

Therefore, we ask ourselves: Who comprises this new group that allows us to speak of a fourth wave of new evangelization taking place today? The answer is the secularized, and in some ways, post-Christian, Western world. This specification, which already emerged in the documents of John Paul II, became explicit in the teaching of Benedict XVI. In his *motu proprio* titled *Ubicumque et semper*, in which he established the Pontifical Council for Promoting the New Evangelization, he speaks of many countries, of "Churches of ancient Christian origin . . . [that] seem particularly resistant to many aspects of the Christian message."[1]

Parallel to the appearance of a new world to evangelize, we have also witnessed a new class of evangelizers emerging each time: bishops during the first three centuries (especially in the third), monks during the second wave, and friars in the third. Even today we are witnessing the emergence of a new category of protagonists of evangelization: the laity. This obviously does not mean replacing one category with another, but rather adding a new component of the people of God to the other, while the bishops, headed by the Pope, always remain the authoritative guides and are ultimately responsible for the missionary task of the Church.

2. Like the wake of a great ship

I said that throughout the centuries the recipients of the message have changed but not the message itself. I must clarify this statement. It is true that the essence of the proclamation cannot change; however, the way of presenting it, its priorities, and the departure point of the message itself can and must change.

Let us summarize the unfolding of the Gospel message up to our present era. First came the announcement made by Jesus, which has as its central theme the news that "the kingdom of God has come near." This unique and unrepeatable stage, which we call the "time of Jesus," was followed after Easter by the "time of the Church." In this second stage, Jesus was no longer the announcer, but the one announced; the word "Gospel" no longer meant (except in the four Gospels) "the Good News brought *by* Jesus," but the Good News *about* Jesus. It had as its object Jesus himself, and, in particular, his death and resurrection. This is what Saint Paul always meant by the word "Gospel."

It is important, however, to be careful not to excessively separate the two "times" from the two announcements—that of Jesus and that of the Church, or (as some have been saying) the "historical Jesus" from the "Christ of faith." Jesus is not only the object of the Church's proclamation, that which is announced. Woe to us if we reduce him to only this! That would mean to "objectify" him and deny the resurrection. In the Church's proclamation, it is the risen Christ who, with his Spirit, still speaks today. He is also the subject who announces. As a text of the Second Vatican Council says, "[Christ] is present in his word, since it is he himself who speaks when the Holy Scriptures are read in the Church."[2]

Starting with the original announcement, we can summarize the successive unfolding of the preaching of the Church with an image suggested by Péguy. Consider the wake of a great ship: it begins in a point, which is the bow of the ship. But it continues to broaden more and more, until it is lost in the horizon and touches the two opposite shores of the sea.[3] This is what came about through the Church's proclamation: it began with a point—the *kerygma*: Christ "was handed over to death for our trespasses and was raised for our justification" (see Rom 4:25; 1 Cor 15:3); and, expressed in an even more emphatic and concise manner, "Jesus is Lord" (see Acts 2:36; Rom 10:9).

The initial expansion of this point occurred with the appearance of the four Gospels (written to explain that initial core), and then with the rest of the New Testament. Then came the Tradition of the Church with its magisterial teaching, liturgy, theology, institutions, laws, and spirituality. The end result is an immense patrimony, which suggests precisely the wake of a ship at its maximum expansion.

At this point, if we want to re-evangelize the post-Christian world, we must make a choice. Where should we begin—at any point along the wake, or from its beginning? The immense abundance of doctrine and institutions can become a handicap if we try to present this to the person who has lost all contact with the Church and no longer knows who Jesus is. It would be like vesting a child all at once with one of those old, huge, heavy brocaded liturgical copes. It would crush him.

Instead, we must help these people establish a relationship with Jesus. We need to do with them what Peter did on the day of Pentecost with the three thousand people present: speak to them about this crucified Jesus whom God raised up. We should take them to the point at which they, too, cut to the heart, shall ask, "Brothers, what should we do?" Then, we shall respond with the words of Peter, "Repent, and be baptized" (Acts 2:37ff.), if you are not yet baptized, or confess, if you already have been.

How and when to do this will depend on our creative ability. And it can vary, as happened in the New Testament: from Peter's discourse to the large crowd on the day of Pentecost, or person to person, like Philip to the Ethiopian eunuch of Queen Candace (see Acts 8:27). Those who shall respond to the announcement will unite, as they did then, around the community of believers. They will listen to the teaching of the apostles and partake in the breaking of bread. Depending on the call and response of each person, little by little they will make their own that entire immense heritage born of the *kerygma*. People will not accept Jesus based on the word of the Church, but they will accept the Church based on the word of Jesus.

We have an ally in this effort: the failure of all attempts by the secular world to replace the Christian *kerygma* with other "screams" and "manifestos." I often use the example of the famous painting by the Norwegian artist Edvard Munch, called *The Scream*. A man stands on a bridge with a reddish background. His hands are wrapped around his wide open mouth, from which he emits a cry. We immediately understand that it is an empty cry full of anguish, without words, only sound. This image seems to me the most effective way to describe the situation of modern humanity. Having cast aside the cry full of substance—the *kerygma*—humanity now finds itself having to scream its existential angst in the dark.

3. Christ, our contemporary

Now I would like to try to explain why it is possible to begin anew in Christianity at any moment from the point of the ship, without deceiving ourselves or simply digging up the past. The reason is straightforward: the ship still sails the sea and its wake still begins with one point!

The philosopher Søren Kierkegaard said some truly wonderful things about the faith and about Jesus, yet on one topic I do not agree with him. One of his favorite themes is that of the contemporaneity of Christ. But he understands such contemporaneity to mean that *we* should be contemporaries of Christ. "He who believes in Christ," he writes, "is obligated to be contemporaneous with him in his humbling of himself."[4] The idea is that in order to really believe with the same faith required of the apostles, we must disregard two thousand years of history and testimony about Christ and put ourselves in the shoes of those to whom Jesus spoke, when he said, for example, "Come to me, all you that are weary and are carrying heavy burdens, and I will give you rest" (Mt 11:28). What would we think of a man who says this, while knowing that he does not have a stone on which to lay his head?

No. I think that the true contemporaneity of Christ is something else. It is *he* who makes himself our contemporary, because, having risen, he lives in the Spirit and in the Church. If we were to make ourselves contemporaries of Christ, it would be merely an intentional contemporaneity; if it is Christ who makes himself our contemporary, it is a real contemporaneity. According to a bold idea of Orthodox spirituality, "anamnesis, that is, liturgical memorial, is a joyous remembrance that makes the past more present than when it was lived." This is not an exaggeration. In the liturgical celebration of the Mass, the event of the death and resurrection of Christ becomes more real for me than it was to those who were actually physically present at the event: at that time, there was a presence "according to the flesh," while now, after the resurrection and Pentecost, the presence is "according to the Spirit."*

The same thing happens when one proclaims with faith, "[The Lord] was handed over to death for our trespasses and was raised for our justification" (Rom 4:25). A fourth-century author writes: "For every man, the beginning of life is that moment when Christ was sacrificed for him. But Christ is sacrificed for him at the moment when he recognizes the grace and becomes conscious of the life procured for him by that sacrifice."[5]

I realize that these things are difficult and perhaps not even possible to say to people, let alone to those in our secularized world. But we who evangelize must be very clear about this in order to draw courage from and believe in the words of John the Evangelist who says, "for the one who is in you is greater than the one who is in the world" (1 Jn 4:4).

4. The laity, new protagonists of evangelization

I said at the beginning of this chapter that lay people are the new protagonists in the present phase of evangelization. Their role in evangelization has been acknowledged by the Council in *Apostolicam Actuositatem* (*Decree on the Apostolate of the Laity*, November 18, 1965), by Pope Paul VI in *Evangelii Nuntiandi* (*On Evangelization in the Modern World*, December 8, 1975),

---

* The author is probably referring to the crowd of spectators, since certainly the Blessed Virgin Mary was present with faith "according to the Spirit." *Ed.*

and by John Paul II in *Christifideles Laici* (*The Lay Members of Christ's Faithful People*, December 30, 1988).

The basis of this universal call to mission is already present in the Gospel. After commissioning the first apostles, we read in the Gospel of Luke, Jesus "appointed seventy others and sent them on ahead of him in pairs to every town and place where he himself intended to go" (Lk 10:1). Those seventy-two disciples were probably all he had gathered by that point, or at least all those who were willing to make a serious commitment to him. Jesus, therefore, sends *all* his disciples.

I once met a layman in the United States who, besides being a father of a family and having a profession, also strove intensely to evangelize. He had a great sense of humor, and he often spoke to audiences in such a way that they would roar in laughter (so typical of Americans). Whenever he would go to a new place, he would start out by saying (quite seriously), "Twenty-five hundred bishops gathered at the Vatican and they asked me to come and preach the Gospel to you." The people would naturally become curious. He would then explain that the twenty-five hundred bishops were those who had taken part in the Second Vatican Council and had written the Decree on the Apostolate of the Laity, which urges every Christian layperson to participate in the evangelizing mission of the Church. He was perfectly correct in saying, "They asked *me*. . . ." Those words of the Council were not spoken as if to the wind—to everyone and no one—but they were personally addressed to each lay Catholic.

Today we know that nuclear energy is released from the "fission" of an atom. An atom of uranium is bombarded and "broken" in two by the collision of a particle called the neutron. This process releases energy and starts a chain reaction. The two new elements are fissile, that is, in turn they split into two other atoms. These, then, split into four and so on until there are billions of atoms, "liberating" an immense amount of energy. This energy is not necessarily destructive because nuclear energy also can be used for peaceful purposes to benefit humanity.

We can use this analogy on a spiritual level to say that the laity are a kind of nuclear energy within the Church. A layperson who is inflamed by the Gospel, by living near others, can "spread" to two more, who then spread to another four. And since lay Christians number not just in the tens of thousands (like the clergy) but in the hundreds of millions, they can truly play a decisive role in spreading the light of the Gospel throughout the world. What makes the evangelization of the laity even more praiseworthy is that it is often done freely, by spending money out of their own pockets.

The apostolate of the laity was discussed even before the Second Vatican Council. The element that the Council introduced regarding this matter, however, was the title used to describe how the laity contribute to the apostolate of the hierarchy. Laypersons are not merely "collaborators" called upon to give of their time, professional abilities, and resources; they are bearers of their own charisms by which, *Lumen Gentium* says, "[The Holy Spirit] makes them fit and ready to undertake the various tasks and offices that contribute toward the renewal and building up of the Church."[6]

Jesus wanted his apostles to be shepherds of the flock and fishers of men. For members of the clergy, it is often easier to be pastors and not fishermen, that is, to nourish with the Word and sacraments those who already come to church, rather than go out in search of those who are far away and live in the most diverse environments. The parable of the lost sheep is reversed today: ninety-nine sheep have strayed and only one remains in the sheepfold (see Mt 18:12). The danger is that we spend all our time nourishing the remaining one and have no time (due in part to the lack of clergy) to go out and search for the lost ones. To this end, the contribution of the laity seems providential.

The most advanced achievement in this regard is represented by the ecclesial movements. Their specific contribution to evangelization is to provide adults with the opportunity to rediscover their baptism and become active and committed members of the Church. Many conversions today, both of nonbelievers and of nominal Christians returning to the practice of their faith, are made in the context of these movements.

Benedict XVI stressed the importance of the family in view of evangelization, speaking of a "leading role" of Christian families in this matter. "And just as the eclipse of God and the crisis of the family are linked," he said, "so the new evangelization is inseparable from the Christian family."[7] Saint Gregory the Great, while commenting on the aforementioned passage of the seventy-two disciples, wrote that Jesus sent them out two by two "because when there are less than two people, there can be no love," and love is that by which Jesus's followers are recognized as his disciples. This applies to everyone, but especially to two parents. If they can no longer do anything to help their children in the faith, they would do much if their children, in observing them, could say to one another: "Look how much Mom and Dad love each other." Scripture says, "Love is from God" (1 Jn 4:7), and this explains why wherever there is a little true love, God is always proclaimed there.

The first evangelization begins within the walls of the home. To one young man who asked what he must do to be saved, Jesus responded, "go, sell what you own, and give the money to the poor . . . ; then come, follow me" (Mk 10:21). But to another young man who wanted to leave everything in order to follow him, Jesus did not permit him, but told him instead, "Go home to your friends, and tell them how much the Lord has done for you, and what mercy he has shown you" (Mk 5:19).

There is a famous African American spiritual entitled, "There Is a Balm in Gilead." Some of its words can encourage the laity (and not only them) in the task of evangelizing—person to person, door to door. The hymn says: "If you cannot sing like angels, if you cannot preach like Paul, go home and tell your neighbor, he died to save us all."

It may comfort our lay brothers and sisters to remember that, besides Mary and Joseph, only their representatives—the shepherds and the Magi—were around the crib of Jesus. Christmas brings us back to the tip of the ship's wake because it all started with a child lying in the manger. "The birth of Christ marks the beginning of the Christian people; the birthday of its Head is the birthday of its body."[8] In the Christmas liturgy we hear proclaimed, "Today Christ is born: today the Savior appeared."

On hearing these words, let us think back to what was said before regarding *anamnesis*, which makes the event more present than when it first happened. Yes, Christ is born today, because he truly is born for me the moment in which I recognize and believe in the mystery. "What good would it be to me that Christ was once born in Bethlehem to Mary, if he were not born again through faith in my heart?" These words, spoken by Origen, were repeated by Saint Augustine and Saint Bernard.[9] They also apply to us.

CHAPTER 5

"What Are Human Beings That You Are Mindful of Them?"

The challenge of
atheistic scientism

In this chapter, I would like to continue reflecting on evangelization in today's era by considering some of the major challenges that proclaiming the Gospel encounters in our secularized world: atheistic scientism, rationalism, and secularism. We shall try to highlight the answer that the Christian faith allows us to give to each one. To this end, I will refer often to the thought of John Henry Newman, not only because the Church recently beatified him, but above all because he spoke directly and addressed the issue of the relationship between faith and modernity with much foresight.

1. The argument of atheistic scientism

To understand what is meant by the term "scientism," it is useful to start from a description given by John Paul II:

> This is the philosophical notion which refuses to admit the validity of forms of knowledge other than those of the positive sciences; and it relegates religious, theological, ethical, and aesthetic knowledge to the realm of mere fantasy. In the past, the same idea emerged in positivism and neo-positivism, which considered metaphysical statements to be meaningless. . . . The undeniable triumphs of scientific research and contemporary technology have helped to propagate a scientistic outlook, which now seems boundless, given its inroads into different cultures and the radical changes it has brought.[1]

We can thus summarize the main arguments of this school of thought.

First argument: *Science (in particular, cosmology, physics, and biology) is the only objective and serious way of knowing reality.* "Modern societies," Jacques Monod wrote, "are built upon science. They owe it their wealth, power, and the certainty that still greater riches and powers will be accessible to man in the future, if he should want it. . . . . Equipped with all power, gifted with all the riches that science offers them, our societies are still trying to live by and teach value systems that have already been undermined by science itself."2

Second argument: *This form of knowledge is incompatible with faith, which is based on assumptions that are neither provable nor falsifiable.* In this field, one scientist has gone so far as to declare "illiterate" any other scientists who profess to be believers, forgetting in this way how many other scientists, much more famous than him, declare themselves to be believers.

Third argument: *Science has proven the falsity, or at least the lack of necessity, of the hypothesis of God.* This assertion was widely covered by the worldwide media on the publication of the book, *The Grand Design*, by the famous English astrophysicist Stephen Hawking. Contrary to what he had previously written, in his new book Hawking argues that knowledge gained from physics has rendered useless the belief in a divine creator of the universe. "Spontaneous creation is the reason there is something rather than nothing, why the universe exists, why we exist," he said.3

Fourth argument: *Almost all—or at least the vast majority— of scientists are atheist.* This is the assertion of militant scientific atheism, whose most active propagator is Richard Dawkins, author of *The God Delusion.*

All these arguments are proven false, not on the basis of *a priori* reasoning or arguments based on theology or faith, but by looking at the results of science itself, as well as the opinions of many of the most illustrious scientists of the past and present. A scientist no less than Max Planck, the founder of the theory of quantum mechanics, said of science what Augustine, Thomas Aquinas, Pascal, Kierkegaard, and others had claimed regarding reason: "Science leads to a point beyond which it can no longer guide."4

I will not insist on rebutting these arguments because this has already been done by scientists and philosophers of science with a skill that I do not have.[5] I will limit myself to a basic observation. During the week in which the media reported on the aforementioned assertion—according to which science had rendered useless the idea of a creator—I had to explain in a Sunday homily to some very simple Christians the fundamental error of these atheistic scientists, and why the people should not let themselves be influenced by the sensation caused by such assertions. I did so with an example that may be useful to repeat here.

Some nocturnal birds, such as the owl, have eyes made for seeing at night in the dark, not during the day. The sun's light would blind them. These birds know everything and move at ease in the nocturnal world, yet they know nothing of the daytime world. Let's adopt, for a moment, the genre of the fable where animals speak to one another. Let's suppose that an eagle made friends with a family of owls and spoke to them about the sun—how it illuminates everything, how, without it, everything would fall into darkness and cold, how their own nocturnal world would not even exist without the sun. Would not the owl answer, "What you say is nonsense! We have never seen your sun. We get along very well, and we get our food without it. Your sun is a useless theory and therefore does not exist."

This is exactly what atheistic scientists do when they say, "God does not exist." They judge a world that they do not know; they apply their laws to something that is out of their reach. In order to see God, one must look with a different eye; one must venture out at night. In this sense, the ancient statement of the psalmist remains valid, "Fools say in their hearts, 'There is no God'" (Ps 14:1).

It is clear that the two sides can reverse themselves and believers could themselves become night birds. This can happen if they claim to judge the results of science based on the principles of their faith, as happened, for example, in the case of Galileo.

2. No to scientism, yes to science

The rejection of scientism should not naturally lead us to refute science or distrust it. To do otherwise would wrong the faith, even before wronging science. History has painfully taught us where such attitudes can lead.

Blessed John Henry Newman has given us a shining example of an open and constructive attitude toward science. Nine years after Darwin published his work on the evolution of species, when more than a few souls around Newman were disturbed and perplexed, he was reassuring. He expressed an opinion that anticipated by a century and a half the Church's present judgment on the compatibility of such a theory with biblical faith. It is worth reading some central passages of his letter to Canon John Walker:

> I do not fear the theory [of evolution]. . . . It does not seem to me to follow that creation is denied because the Creator, millions of years ago, gave laws to matter. . . . We do not deny or circumscribe the Creator, because we hold he has created the self-acting originating human mind, which has almost a creative gift; much less then do we deny or circumscribe his power if we hold that he gave matter such laws as by their blind instrumentality molded and constructed through innumerable ages the world as we see it. . . . Mr. Darwin's theory *need* not then to be atheistical, be it true or not; it may simply be suggesting a larger idea of Divine Prescience and Skill. . . . I do not [see] that "the accidental evolution of organic beings"

is inconsistent with divine design—it is accidental to *us*, not to *God*.6

Newman's great faith allowed him to look with great serenity at present and future scientific discoveries. "When then a flood of facts, ascertained or suspected, comes pouring in upon us, with a multitude of others in prospect, all believers in revelation, be they Catholic or not, are roused to consider their bearing upon themselves."7 He saw in such scientific discoveries of the age "an indirect relation with religious opinions." An example of this relation, I think, is precisely the fact that during the same period in which Darwin penned his theory on the evolution of species, Newman independently stated his doctrine on the "development of Christian doctrine." Alluding to the analogy, on this point, between the natural or physical order and the moral one, he wrote: "As the Creator rested on the seventh day from the work which he had made, yet he 'worketh hitherto'; so he gave the Creed once for all in the beginning, yet blesses its growth still, and provides for its increase."8

The Pontifical Academy of Sciences is a concrete expression of the new and positive attitude on the part of the Catholic Church toward science. Eminent scientists from around the world—believers and nonbelievers alike—come together there to present and freely debate their ideas on problems of common interest regarding science and faith.

3. Man for the cosmos, or the cosmos for man?

I repeat that it is not my intention here to engage in a general critique of scientism. I wish, however, to highlight a particular aspect of it, one that has a direct and decisive influence on evangelization, that is, the position of the human race in the vision of atheistic scientism.

By now there is practically a competition among nonbelieving scientists—especially biologists and cosmologists—to see who can best assert the total marginalization and insignificance of the human race in the universe and life itself. Monod wrote: "The ancient covenant is broken, and man finally knows that he is alone in the immensity of the universe, from which he emerged by chance. His duty, as his destiny, is not written anywhere." 9 Another person wrote: "I have always believed that I am insignificant. While knowing the dimensions of the universe, I do but realize how true this is. . . . We are just a speck of mud on a planet that belongs to the sun."10

In this regard the goal of a future universe without the presence of human beings has come to be assumed and even desired. This is called "deep ecology." This can be seen, for example, in the website of the Voluntary Human Extinction Movement, which favors the voluntary extinction of the human species in order to allow other species to develop without the violent intervention of the human race.

Blaise Pascal refuted this view in advance with an argument that no one has yet been able (nor ever will be able) to disprove:

> Man is but a reed, the most feeble thing in nature, but he is a thinking reed. The entire universe need not arm itself to crush him. A vapor, a drop of water suffices to kill him. But, if the universe were to crush him, man would still be more noble than that which killed him, because he knows that he dies and the advantage which the universe has over him; the universe knows nothing of this.11

Together with humanity, this scientistic vision of reality suddenly removes even Christ from the center of the universe. He is reduced, to use the words of Maurice Blondel, "to an historical accident, isolated from the cosmos as an intruder or someone lost in the vast and hostile immensity of the universe."12

This vision of humanity is beginning to be reflected in practical terms at the level of culture and mentality. Certain excesses in environmentalism are now attempting to equate the rights of animals with those of people. It is well-known that some pets are cared for and fed much better than millions of children. The influence of this vision is also felt in the religious field. In some widespread forms of religiosity, contact and harmony with the energy of the cosmos have taken the place of contact with God as the way of salvation. What Paul said of God, "In him we live and move and have our being" (Acts 17:28), is now being said of the material cosmos.

In some aspects, this is a return to the pre-Christian ethos that had as its basic scheme *God—cosmos—humanity,* and against which the Bible and Christianity countered with *God—humanity—cosmos.* In other words, the cosmos is for humanity, not humanity for the cosmos. One of the most violent accusations that Celsus, the pagan philosopher, addressed to Jews and Christians was directed against their belief that "there is a God, and immediately after him, we who are made by him and are altogether like unto God, and that all things have been made subject to us—earth, and water, and air, and stars—and that all things exist for our sake, and are ordained to be subject to us."[13]

But there is also a profound difference between Celsus and the modern accusers of Christianity. In ancient thought—especially Greek—humanity, though subordinate to the cosmos, was still held in the highest dignity. This is highlighted in the masterful work by Max Pohlenz, *The Greek Man.*[14] Today, instead, it seems that some take delight in leveling humanity, stripping it of any claim to superiority over the rest of nature. Rather than an "atheistic humanism," at least from this point of view, one would speak of, in my opinion, an antihumanism or even an "atheistic dishumanism."

Now we come to the Christian vision. Celsus did not err in deriving his understanding of Christianity from the great pronouncement of Genesis 1:26 on the creation of the human race "in Our [God's] image and likeness."[15] The biblical vision has found its most beautiful expression in Psalm 8:3–6:

> When I look at your heavens, the work of your fingers,
> the moon and the stars that you have established;
> what are human beings that you are mindful of them,
> mortals that you care for them?
> Yet you have made them a little lower than God,
> and crowned them with glory and honor.
> You have given them dominion over the works of your hands;
> you have put all things under their feet. . . .

Saint Paul completes this vision, indicating the place that the person of Christ occupies in it, "The world or life or death or the present or the future—all belong to you, and you belong to Christ, and Christ belongs to God" (1 Cor 3:22–23).

The creation of humanity in the image of God has certain implications regarding the concept of humanity that the current debate forces us to bring to light. Everything is based on the revelation of the Trinity that Christ brought. Humanity is created in the image of God, meaning that it shares in the intimate essence of God, which is a relationship of love between the Father, Son, and Holy Spirit. Only humanity, inasmuch as people are capable of relationships, can participate in the personal and relational dimension of God.

This means that human beings, in their essence, even if at a creaturely level, are that which the Father, the Son, and the Holy Spirit are in their essence at the uncreated level. The human person is "person" precisely because of this intimate relational core, which renders the person able to receive the relationship that God wishes to establish with humanity, and at the same time generate relations toward others and toward the world. Clearly there is an ontological gap between God and the human creature; nevertheless, by grace (and never forget this distinction!) this gap is filled so that it is less profound than the one that exists between humanity and the rest of creation.

4. The force of truth

Let's now try to see how to translate this Christian vision of the relationship between humanity and the cosmos into the field of evangelization. But first, a premise. Dionysius the Areopagite stated this great truth: "One does not have to refute the opinions of others, nor should one write against an opinion or a religion that does not seem good. One has to write only in favor of the truth, and not against others."[16]

This principle should not be made absolute (sometimes it is useful and necessary to refute false doctrines), but it is certain that the positive exposition of the truth is often more effective than the refutation of its opposite error. I believe that it is important to take into account this criterion in evangelization and, in particular, against the three aforementioned obstacles: scientism, secularism, and rationalism. In evangelization, peaceful exposure to the Christian vision—while relying on its inherent strength accompanied by personal conviction—is more effective than arguing against others' false opinions and errors. And it should always be done, as Saint Peter persistently instructed, "with gentleness and reverence" (1 Pet 3:16).

According to the Christian vision, the highest expression of the dignity and vocation of humanity is crystallized in the doctrine of the deification of the human person. This doctrine has had a different emphasis in Orthodoxy and in the Western Churches. The Greek Fathers made it the central point of their spirituality, despite all the baggage that pagan use had brought to the concept of deification (*theosis*). Latin theology has insisted less on it. "The purpose of life for Greek Christians is deification, while for Western Christians it is the acquisition of holiness. . . . According to the Greeks, the Word was made flesh to restore to man the likeness to God lost in Adam in order to deify him. According to the Latins, he became man to redeem the human race . . . and to pay the debt owed to the righteousness of God."[17] We might say, at the risk of oversimplifying, that Latin theology, following Saint Augustine, insists more on what Christ came to take away: sin. Greek theology, on the other hand, insists more on what he came to give to humanity: the image of God, the Holy Spirit, and divine life.

This distinction should not be overemphasized, as some Orthodox writers tend to do. Latin spirituality sometimes expresses the same ideal, even if in general it avoids the term "deification," which, it is worth recalling, is not used in biblical language. One can think of the vibrant exhortation of Saint Leo the Great, who expresses the same image of the Christian vocation: "Christian, recognize your dignity and, now that you share in God's own nature, do not return to your former base condition by sinning. Remember who is your Head and of whose body you are a member."[18]

Unfortunately, some Orthodox authors have remained stuck in the controversies of the fourteenth century between Gregory of Palamas and Barlaam, and they seem to ignore the rich Latin mystical tradition. The teachings of Saint John of the Cross, for example, tell us that the Christian, having been redeemed by Christ and made a child of God through the Son, is immersed in the flow of Trinitarian actions. Thus, the Christian participates in the intimate life of God in a manner no less elevated than that of deification, even if expressed in different terms. Also, the doctrine on the Holy Spirit's gifts of knowledge and wisdom, so dear to Saint Bonaventure and other medieval authors, was inspired by the same mystical inspiration. The doctrine and the term deification (*deificari*), are present, for example, in Saint Bernard, who sees it as the last degree of God's love in the treatise, *De Deo diligendo*.

One cannot, however, fail to recognize that Orthodox spirituality has something to teach the rest of Christendom on this point—to Protestant theology even more than Catholic theology. If there is, in fact, something truly opposed to the Orthodox vision of the Christian deified by grace, it would be the Protestant conception (in particular Lutheran), of extrinsic or legal justification, by which redeemed humanity is "at the same time righteous and a sinner," a sinner in himself, righteous before God.

Above all, we can learn from the Eastern tradition not to limit this sublime ideal of Christian life to a spiritual elite called to mystical life, but to propose it to all the baptized and make it the object of catechesis to people, and of religious formation in seminaries and novitiates. In my years of formation, there was an almost exclusive insistence on an asceticism centering on correcting vices and acquiring virtues. The Russian saint, Seraphim of Sarov, responded without hesitation to a disciple's question on the ultimate goal of the Christian life: "The true aim of the Christian life is the acquisition of the Holy Spirit of God. Prayer, fasting, vigils, almsgiving, and every other good deed done in the name of Christ are only means of acquiring the Holy Spirit."[19]

5. "All things came into being through him"

We must continually remind ourselves and others of this ideal, which is the common patrimony of Christendom. It is from the Incarnation of the Word that the Greek Fathers derived the very possibility of divinization. Saint Athanasius never tired of repeating, "The Word became man so that we might be deified."[20] "He became incarnate and man became God, because he is united to God," wrote Saint Gregory Nazianzus in turn.[21] With Christ, being "in the image of God" is restored, or brought back to light, and this establishes the superiority of humanity over the rest of creation.

I mentioned earlier how the marginalization of human beings automatically brings with it the marginalization of Christ from the cosmos and history. Even from this point of view, the Incarnation is the most radical antithesis to the vision of scientism. John proclaims: "All things came into being through him, and without him not one thing came into being" (1:3), and Paul writes: "all things have been created through him and for him" (Col 1:16). The Church has taken up this revelation, and we say in the Creed, *"Per quem omnia facta sunt"* ("through him all things were made"). It can undoubtedly shock us to listen again to these words while all around we only hear: "The world is self-explanatory, and there is no need of the hypothesis of a creator," or "we are the fruit of chance and necessity." But it is easier for conversion and faith to spring from a shock of this kind than from a prolonged argument in defense of the faith.

The crucial question is this: Will we, who aspire to re-evangelize the world, be able to increase our faith to these mind-boggling dimensions? Do we really believe with all our heart that "all things were made through Christ and for Christ"? In his book, *Introduction to Christianity*, the professor (at that time) Joseph Ratzinger wrote:

> It is only in the second section of the Creed that we come up against the real difficulty—already considered briefly in the introduction—about Christianity: the profession of faith that the man Jesus, an individual executed in Palestine around about the year 30, the "Christus" (anointed, chosen) of God, indeed God's own Son, is the central and decisive point of all human history. It seems both presumptuous and foolish to assert that one single figure who is bound to disappear farther and farther into the mists of the past is the authoritative center of all history?[22]

We answer these questions without hesitation: yes, it is possible, it is freeing, and it is joyous, not by our own strength but by the priceless gift of faith that we have received and for which we give infinite thanks to God.

CHAPTER 6

"Always Be Ready to Make Your Defense to Anyone Who Demands an Accounting from You"

The challenge to rationalism

1. The usurpation of reason

Rationalism is the second obstacle that makes so much of modern culture resist the Gospel. We intend to address that problem in this chapter.

Cardinal (now Blessed) John Henry Newman has left us a memorable sermon delivered on December 11, 1831, at the University of Oxford. Its title, "The Usurpation of Reason" (that is, the misuse or abuse of the power of reason), already defines what is meant by rationalism.[1] In a commentary on this speech, written as a note in the preface of the third edition of the Oxford Sermons in 1871, the author explains his meaning. He said that by "usurpation of reason," he meant

> a certain popular abuse of the faculty; viz., when it occupies itself upon Religion, without a due familiar acquaintance with its subject-matter, or without a use of the first principles proper to it. This so-called Reason is in Scripture designated "the wisdom of the world"; that is, the reasoning of secular minds about Religion, or reasonings about Religion based upon secular maxims, which are intrinsically foreign to it.[2]

In another of his university sermons, titled "Faith and Reason, Contrasted as Habits of Mind," Newman uses the analogy of conscience to show why reason cannot be the final judge in matters of religion and faith:

> No one will say that Conscience is against Reason, or that its dictates cannot be thrown into an argumentative form; yet who will, therefore, maintain that it is not an original principle, but must depend, before it acts, upon some previous processes of Reason? Reason analyzes the grounds and motives of action: a reason is an analysis, but is not the motive itself. As, then, Conscience is a simple element in our nature, yet its operations admit of being surveyed and scrutinized by Reason; so may Faith be cognizable, and its acts be justified, by Reason, without therefore being, in matter of fact,

dependent upon it. . . . When the Gospel is said to require a rational Faith, this need not mean more than that Faith is accordant to right Reason in the abstract, not that it results from it in the particular case.[3]

Newman uses another analogy regarding art. He writes, "As then the critic ascertains what he cannot himself create, so Reason may put its sanction upon the acts of Faith, without in consequence being the source from which Faith springs."[4]

Newman's analysis offers some new and original thoughts. He highlights reason's imperialist tendency, so to speak, to subject every aspect of reality to its own principles. One can, however, also consider rationalism from another point of view, strictly connected with the previous one. While maintaining the "political" metaphor Newman used, we could define it as an attitude of isolationism, of enclosure within reason itself. It does not consist so much of invading another field, as of not recognizing the existence of any other field outside its own. In other words, it consists in refusing to acknowledge that there can be any truth outside of what passes through human reason. In this role, rationalism is not a fruit of the Enlightenment (even if that movement accelerated it, with its effects enduring until today). Rationalism is a tendency that faith has always had to struggle against, not only the Christian faith, but also the Jewish and Islamic faiths, at least during the Middle Ages.

In every age, voices have risen up against this pretension of reason's absolutism, and not only from men of faith, but also from men engaged in the field of reason itself—philosophers and scientists. "The supreme act of reason," Pascal wrote, "is to recognize that there are infinite things that lie beyond it."[5] The very instant reason recognizes its own limits, it breaks and exceeds them. This acknowledgment is produced by the work of reason itself, which makes it, therefore, an exquisitely rational act. It is, literally, a "learned ignorance,"[6] an ignorance for good reason, knowing that it does not know.

It must, therefore, be said that whoever does not recognize the capacity of reason to transcend itself sets a limit on it and, thus, humiliates it. Kierkegaard once wrote:

> So far, people have always spoken thus, "To say that one cannot understand this or that thing does not satisfy science that wants to understand." This is a mistake. One should say, in fact, the opposite: If human science does not want to recognize that there is something it cannot understand, or—in a still more precise manner—something which it can clearly "understand that it cannot understand," then everything is unsettled. Therefore, it remains a task of human knowledge to understand that there are things—and what those things are—that it cannot understand.[7]

2. Faith and the sense of the sacred

We should expect this type of reciprocal dispute between faith and reason to continue well into the future. It is inevitable that people of every age will take it up again. Yet, neither the rationalists will convert believers with their arguments, nor believers the rationalists. We need to find a way to break this cycle and free faith from these limitations. In all this debate on reason and faith, it is reason that imposes its field of choice and compels faith, so to speak, to play defense as the visiting team.

Cardinal Newman was well aware of this. In another of his university sermons, he warned against the risk of making faith too worldly in its desire to compete against reason. He said that he understood the reasons of those who were tempted to completely separate their faith from a rational search, even if he could not totally accept them. These reasons are due to:

the strife and division to which argument and controversy minister, the proud self-confidence which is fostered by strength of the reasoning powers, the laxity of opinion which often accompanies the study of the evidences, the coldness, the formality, the secular and carnal spirit which is compatible with an exact adherence to dogmatic formularies; and on the other hand, when they recollect that Scripture represents religion as a divine life, seated in the affections and manifested in spiritual graces.[8]

In all Newman's contributions to understanding the relationship between reason and faith, which was no less debated then as today, there was an admonition: rationalism cannot be fought against with another type of rationalism, even if of a contrary kind. We must, therefore, find another way that does not claim to replace the rational defense of the faith but that accompanies it. We should also consider that today's recipients of the Gospel are not represented only by intellectuals (who are able to engage in this type of debate), but also by many ordinary people who are indifferent to these arguments and more sensitive to other approaches.

Pascal proposed the way of the heart: "The heart has its reasons which reason does not know."[9] The romantics (Schleiermacher, for example) proposed the way of sentiment. I believe that another way to proceed is left to us: that of experience and of witness. I do not mean to speak of a personal and subjective experience of faith, at least for now; but rather, a universal and objective experience that can be of value even while confronting people still outside the faith. This does not bring us to the full faith that saves: faith in Jesus Christ who died and rose again. But it can help us to bring about its prerequisite, namely, openness to the mystery—the perception of something that is above the world and beyond reason.

Modern phenomenology of religion—the science that studies the forms religious sentiment takes in different cultures—has made a notable contribution to faith in regard to the traditional belief that something exists that cannot be explained by reason.* Phenomenology has shown that this belief is not a theoretical proposition or a tenet of faith, but is, rather, a primeval fact of experience. This theme has been taken up especially by Rudolf Otto in his classical work, *The Idea of the Holy*.[10] He discusses a certain sentiment that has accompanied humanity since its origins and is present in all religions and cultures. The author calls this sentiment the "numinous," which is a primary fact, irreducible to any other emotion or human experience. This feeling is evoked due to some external or internal circumstance that causes one to tremble at the revelation of the "terrible and awesome" mystery of the supernatural. The numinous manifests itself in varying degrees of purity: from the more primitive stage, which is a troubling reaction stirred up by things like ghost stories or tales of spirits to the more pure stage, which is the manifestation of the holiness of God—the biblical *Qadosh*—as in the great scene of the calling of Isaiah (see Is 6:1ff.).

Saint Augustine long ago anticipated this insight of modern scholars of religious phenomenology. He wrote in his *Confessions*: "When I first knew you, you lifted me up. . . . And you beat back the weakness of my sight, shining forth upon me your dazzling beams of light, and I trembled with love and fear [*contremui amore et horrore*]."[11] He highlighted the suprarational character of his experience: "Who shall comprehend such things and who shall tell of it? What is it that shines through me and strikes my heart without injury, so that I both

---

* The phenomenology of religion refers to the experiential aspect of religion. *Ed.*

shudder and burn? [*Et inhorresco inardesco*] I shudder inasmuch as I am unlike it; I burn inasmuch as I am like it."[12]

Otto uses the adjective "irrational or non-rational" to designate the object of this experience. The subtitle of his work is, "An inquiry into the non-rational factor in the idea of the divine and its relation to the rational." But his entire work also shows that the term "nonrational" does not mean irrational or "contrary to reason," but precisely "nonrational," that is, something that cannot be translated into rational concepts and terms.

If this is so, then the re-evangelization of the secularized world must start with a recovery of a sense of the sacred. The cultural terrain of rationalism—its cause and effect together—is the loss of the sense of the sacred; therefore, it is necessary for the Church to help people to go out and to reclaim and rediscover the presence and beauty of the sacred in the world. Charles Péguy said that "the frightening absence of the Sacred is the most striking feature of the modern world."* This is evident in every aspect of life, but especially in art, literature, and everyday speech. For many artists, to be defined as "desecrating" is no longer an insult but a compliment.

The Bible is sometimes accused of having "desacralized" the world for having driven out pagan beliefs in nymphs and divinities from the mountains, seas, and forests, and for having made natural phenomena interpreted as gods into simple creatures at the service of human beings. This is true, but it is precisely by stripping these things of the false belief that they are gods, that Scripture restored them to their true nature as "signs" of the divine. The Bible does not deny the sacredness of creatures, but only opposes making them into idols.

---

* The source of this quote is not known. *Ed.*

In fact, "secularized" in such a way, creation has even more power to rouse the experience of the numinous and the divine. In my opinion, the famous declaration of Kant—the most illustrious representative of philosophical rationalism—bears the mark of such an experience:

> Two things fill the mind with ever new and increasing admiration and awe, the oftener and the more steadily we reflect on them: *the starry heavens above and the moral law within.* [. . .] The former begins from the place I occupy in the external world of sense, and enlarges my connection therein to an unbounded extent with worlds upon worlds and systems of systems, and moreover into limitless times of their periodic motion, its beginning and continuance.[13]

Francis Collins, a currently active scientist who was recently appointed to the Pontifical Academy of Sciences, wrote a book titled *The Language of God.* In it, he describes the moment of his return to faith: "One beautiful fall morning, as I was hiking in the mountains to the west of the Mississippi for the first time, the majesty and beauty of creation overwhelmed my resistance. I knew that my search had reached an end. The next morning, when the sun came up, I knelt in the wet grass and surrendered to Jesus Christ."[14]

Both scientific and technological discoveries can be events of wonder and experiences of the divine, rather than occasions of disenchantment. The final moment of the discovery of the human genome was described by the same man, Francis Collins, who was at the head of a governmental team that led to the discovery, as "both a stunning scientific achievement and an occasion of worship." Among the wonders of creation, nothing is more magnificent than humanity and, within humanity, human intelligence created by God.

Science by now has lost hope of ever reaching the furthermost limit in its exploration of the infinitely large, namely, the

universe, and of the infinitely small, namely, subatomic parti-
cles. As a result of these "disproportions," some argue that a
creator does not exist, and that human beings are insignificant.
For the believer, however, they are the signs par excellence not
only of the existence of God but also of his attributes. The vastness of the universe is the most adequate sign of the infinite
greatness and transcendence of God, while the smallness of the
atom is a sign of God's immanence and of the humility of the
Incarnation, which led God to become a babe in the womb of
his mother and a tiny piece of bread at the hands of the priest
in the Eucharist.*

Even in everyday human life at times it is possible to have
an experience of "another" dimension: falling in love, the birth
of one's first child, or sentiments of great joy. We must help
people to open their eyes and regain their ability to wonder.
"The person who wonders shall reign," is a saying attributed to
Jesus outside of the Gospel.15 In the novel, *The Brothers Karamazov*, Dostoyevsky relates the words that the monk Zosima
once said while he was still an army officer. Struck by grace, he
renounced on the spot his intent to fight in a duel with his
adversary, saying:

> Gentlemen, look around you at the gifts of God, the clear sky,
> the pure air, the tender grass, the birds; nature is beautiful and
> sinless, and we, only we, are sinful and foolish, and we don't
> understand that life is heaven, for we have only to understand
> that and it will at once be fulfilled in all its beauty, we shall
> embrace each other and weep.16

What a genuine sense of the sacredness of the world and
of life!

---

* That is, the Eucharist has the appearance of bread but the whole substance
of the bread is changed into the Body of Christ. *Ed.*

We Italians are not forced to resort to Russian literature to find descriptions of the experience of the numinous. We have an example in our own language—perhaps the most beautiful in all literature—the poem, *The Infinite*, by Giacomo Leopardi. Read it again, after what we have said, in order to discover something that perhaps we had not noticed when we may have studied it at school:

> I always loved this solitary hill
> And this green hedge that hides on every side
> The last and dim horizon from our view.
> But as I sit and gaze, a never-ending
> Space far beyond it and unearthly silence
> And deepest quiet to my thought I picture,
> And as with terror is my heart o'ercast
> With wondrous awe. And while I hear the wind
> Amid the green leaves rustling, I compare
> That silence infinite to this sound,
> And to my mind eternity occurs.
> And all the vanished ages, and the present
> Whose sound doth meet mine ear. And so in this
> Immensity my thought is drifted on.
> And to be wrecked on such a sea is sweet.[17]

In these verses, we find the entire essence of the "frightening and fascinating" mystery of Rudolf Otto: the aspect of attraction and love ("it is *sweet* to shipwreck in such a sea"), but also that the sacred fear ("my heart scarcely can hide a *fear*"). As Christians, we need only give a name to this "sea." It is the endless ocean, bottomless and without shore, of the love of God.

For believers, the liturgy can be a privileged opportunity to experience the numinous, especially during some of its more powerful moments. From various ancient Easter homilies, such as those of Melito of Sardis of the second century, scholars have coined the expression "cultic epiphany." This designates the experience that Christians had of the living presence of the Risen Lord in their midst at the height of the liturgical action. It is possible that the Aramaic cry, *Maranatha*, when pronounced differently (*Maran atha* instead of *Marana tha*), served precisely to express this collective sentiment: not an invocation "Our Lord, come!" but an exclamation: "The Lord has come! The Lord is here" (see 1 Cor 16:22).

3. In need of witnesses

When the experience of the sacred and the divine that comes to us suddenly and unexpectedly from outside of us is received and developed, it becomes a lived subjective experience. Hence, the "witnesses" of God are the saints and, in a particular way, the mystics.

According to the famous definition of Dionysius the Areopagite, the mystics are those who have "suffered God,"[18] that is, they have experienced and lived the divine. For the rest of humanity, they are like explorers who have gone first and, after having secretly entered the Promised Land, have returned to report what they have seen—"a land that flows with milk and honey"—and to exhort all the people to cross the Jordan (see Num 14:6–9). Through them, while still in this life, the first rays of eternal life come down upon us.

When we read the mystics' writings, the most subtle arguments of atheists and rationalists appear distant, even naive! They evoke a sense of astonishment or even pity, like people speaking of things they clearly do not know. They resemble someone conversing with another person whom they believed was making continual grammatical mistakes, without realizing that the other person was simply speaking a foreign language. Yet, we should have no desire to refute them, as our words spoken in defense of God would appear empty and out of place in these cases.

The mystics are, par excellence, those who have discovered that God "exists," actually; that he alone truly exists and is infinitely more real than what we usually call reality. It was precisely from one of these encounters that a Jewess and convinced atheist, a follower of the philosopher Husserl, discovered the living God one night. I am speaking of Edith Stein, now Saint Teresa Benedicta of the Cross. She had stayed as a guest with some Christian friends who were away one evening, leaving her alone in the house. Not knowing what to do, she took a book from their library and began to read. It was the autobiography of Saint Teresa of Avila. She read it throughout the entire night. When she reached the end, she said simply, "This is the truth!" Early the next morning, she went into town to buy a Catholic catechism and a missal. After studying the texts, she went to a nearby church and asked to be baptized.

I, too, once experienced in a modest way the power that the mystics have to let you touch the supernatural. It was at a time of much discussion about a book by a theologian entitled, *Does God Exist?* (*Existiert Gott?* in the original German). But after reading it, very few were ready to invert the title to *God Does Exist!* While attending a convention on this subject, I brought with me a book of the writings of Blessed Angela of Foligno, with whom I was not yet familiar. It was literally amazing; I would open it and read it during breaks at the conference. At the end, I closed it and said to myself, "Does God exist? Not only does he exist, but he is truly a consuming fire!"

Unfortunately, a certain literary trend has been successful in defusing even the living "proof" of the mystics on the existence of God. But it did so in a remarkable way: not by reducing their number but by increasing them; not by restricting the phenomenon but by greatly expanding it. I am referring to some authors who, in studying the mystics, in creating anthologies of their writings, or in writing their biographies, would place alongside them someone of a totally different type, as if they belonged together. For example, they have paired Saint John of the Cross with Nostradamus; saints with eccentrics; Christian mysticism with medieval Kabbalah, Hermeticism, theosophism, forms of pantheism, and even alchemy.[19] True mystics are in an entirely different category, and the Church has good reason to be quite strict in its discernment of true mysticism.

The theologian Karl Rahner—in taking up, it seems, a phrase of Raimon Panikkar—stated: "The devout Christian of the future will either be a 'mystic,' one who has 'experienced' something, or he will cease to be anything at all."[20] He meant that in order to keep the faith alive in the future, we will need the witness of those who have had a profound experience of God, rather than people who can demonstrate its rational plausibility. When the Apostle Peter exhorted the Christian community to be ready to render an "accounting for the hope that is in you" (1 Pt 3:15), it is clear from the context that he did not intend for them to speak about speculative or dialectical reasons for their hope, but practical reasons, that is, their experience of Christ, united to the apostolic witness that guaranteed it.

Cardinal Newman's motto, *Cor ad cor loquitur,* can be translated from the Latin: "What comes into the heart of people is only what comes forth from the heart of the one announcing." In his fifth university sermon titled "Personal Influence, the Means of Propagating the Truth," Newman writes that the truth "has been upheld in the world not as a system, not by books, not by argument, nor by temporal power, but by the personal influence of such men as have already been described, who are at once the teachers and the patterns of it."21 Paul VI said basically the same thing: "Modern man listens more willingly to witnesses than to teachers, and if he does listen to teachers, it is because they are witnesses."22

4. A leap of faith

I have spoken about sudden outpourings of the numinous and the supernatural in life. It is not just nonbelievers and rationalists who need them in order to come to faith, however; we, as believers, need them too. The greatest danger that religious people risk is reducing the faith to a series of rites and formulas, perhaps repeated scrupulously, but mechanically and without participating intimately with one's entire being. Lamenting in Isaiah, the Lord said: ". . . these people draw near with their mouths and honor me with their lips, while their hearts are far from me, and their worship of me is a human commandment learned by rote" (Is 29:13).

Christmas can be an excellent occasion to make this leap of faith. It is the supreme "theophany" of God, the highest "manifestation of the Sacred." Unfortunately, the phenomenon of secularism is stripping this feast of its character of "fearsome mystery," which leads to holy fear and adoration. Instead, it is being reduced solely to the aspect of "fascinating mystery," but unfortunately "fascinating" only in a natural sense, not a supernatural one: a mere celebration of family values, winter, the evergreen tree, reindeer, and Santa Claus. In some countries, attempts are underway to even change the name of Christmas to a "festival of lights." In only a few cases is secularization more visible than at Christmas.

For me, the "numinous" character of Christmas is linked to

a memory. One year I assisted at a midnight Mass presided over by Saint Pope John Paul II at Saint Peter's Basilica. The moment arrived for the singing of the *Kalenda,* that is, the solemn proclamation of the birth of the Savior, present in the ancient Martyrology and reintroduced into the Christmas liturgy after Vatican II:

> when ages beyond number had run their course from the creation of the world, [. . .]
>
> in the thirteenth century since the People of Israel were led by Moses in the Exodus from Egypt; [. . .]
>
> in the one hundred and ninety-fourth Olympiad;
>
> in the year seven hundred and fifty-two since the foundation of the City of Rome;
>
> in the forty-second year of the reign of Caesar Octavian Augustus, [. . .]
>
> Jesus Christ, eternal God and Son of the eternal Father, [. . .]
>
> was conceived by the Holy Spirit, and when nine months had passed since his conception, was born of the Virgin Mary in Bethlehem of Judah, and was made man.*

When the last words were said, I felt an "anointing of faith": a sudden inner clarity, so that I remember saying to myself: "It is true! Everything they are singing is true! These are not just words; the Eternal actually has entered into time. The last event of the series has broken the series; it has created an irreversible

---

* Although the author is describing a Mass that took place in 2003, the updated Roman Missal 2011 is used. This text, The Nativity of our Lord Jesus Christ, may be chanted or recited, most appropriately on December 24, during the celebration of the Liturgy of the Hours. It may also be chanted or recited before the beginning of Christmas Mass during the Night. (The musical notation is found in Appendix I of the Roman Missal, Third Edition.) *Ed.*

'before' and 'after'; the computation of time, which took place earlier in relation to different events (the Olympics, such and such a kingdom, and so on), now takes place in relation to a single event!" A sudden emotion shot through my entire person, and I could only say, "Thank you, Most Holy Trinity, and thanks be also to you, Holy Mother of God."

In order to make Christmas an occasion for a leap of faith, it helps a great deal to create places and times for silence. The liturgy envelops the birth of Jesus in silence: *dum medium silentium tenerent omnia* ("while gentle silence enveloped all things," Wis 18:14). *"Stille Nacht"* ("Silent Night") is often sung at Christmas as one of the most popular and beloved of all Christmas carols. At Christmas, we should feel as if the invitation of the psalm is personally addressed to us, "Be still, and know that I am God!" (Ps 46:10).

The Mother of God is the unsurpassable model of Christmas silence. It is written, "But Mary treasured all these words and pondered them in her heart" (Lk 2:19). The silence of Mary at Christmas is more than just keeping quiet; it is wonder, it is adoration. It is a "religious silence"—that of being overwhelmed by reality. The most authentic interpretation of the silence of Mary is that of some ancient Byzantine icons, where the Mother of God appears to us still, with her gaze fixed, her eyes wide open, as one who has seen things that cannot be repeated with words. Mary was the first to raise to God what Saint Gregory of Nazianzus calls a "hymn of silence."[23]

CHAPTER 7

We Have Seen and Testify to It, and Declare to You Eternal Life

The Christian response
to secularism

1. Secularization and secularism

In this chapter, we will deal with the third difficulty that evangelization encounters in the modern world: secularization. The Pontifical Council for Promoting the New Evangelization was established by Benedict XVI to be "at the service of the particular Churches, especially in those territories of Christian tradition where the phenomenon of secularization is more obviously apparent."[1]

Secularization is a complex and ambivalent phenomenon. On the one hand, it can indicate the autonomy of worldly realities and the separation of the kingdom of God from the kingdom of Caesar. In this sense, not only is it in accordance with the Gospel, but it actually finds one of its deepest roots there. Secularization, however, can also indicate an entire set of attitudes that are hostile to religion and faith, for which the term "secularism" is preferred. Secularism is to secularization what scientism is to science, and what rationalism is to rationality.

In dealing with the obstacles or challenges that faith encounters in the modern world, we shall refer exclusively to this negative sense of secularization. Limited to that sense, the phenomenon of secularization has many faces depending on the field in which it manifests itself: theology, science, ethics, biblical hermeneutics, everyday life, and culture in general. Here I shall use the term based on its most ancient meaning. The word secularization (like secularism) derives, in fact, from the Latin word, *saeculum*, which in our common language has come to indicate the present time—"the current age," according to the Bible (see Eph 1:21; 2 Tim 4:10; Mt 12:32). This meaning is opposed to eternity—the future age, or *saecula saeculorum*, "world without end" of Scripture (see for example, Gal 1:5; Eph

3:21). In this sense, secularism is synonymous with temporality, or the reduction of reality solely to the earthly dimension.

The decline of a mindset that considers eternity has had the same effect on the Christian faith that sand has when thrown on a flame: it stifles and extinguishes it. Faith in eternal life constitutes one of the conditions that makes evangelization possible. "If for this life only we have hoped in Christ, we are of all people most to be pitied" (1 Cor 15:19).

2. The rise and decline of belief in eternity

Let us briefly recall the history of belief in life after death. This will help us to appreciate the originality that the Gospel brought to this idea. In the Hebrew religion of the Old Testament, such a belief was affirmed only belatedly. It was only after their exile, in the face of failure of their temporal hopes and expectations, that the idea of the resurrection of the flesh and the reward for the righteous after death gained ground. Yet even then, this idea was not accepted by all (the Sadducees, for example, did not share such a belief).

This resoundingly refutes the arguments of those (for example, Feuerbach, Marx, Freud) who have explained belief in God with the desire for an eternal reward, as if it were a projection of dashed earthly expectations on the afterlife. Israel believed in God for many centuries before they believed in an eternal reward in the afterlife! It was not, therefore, the desire for an eternal reward that produced belief in God, but faith in God that produced belief in an otherworldly reward.

Biblically, the full revelation of eternal life is had with the coming of Christ. Jesus does not establish the certainty of eternal life on the nature of humanity (the immortality of the soul), but on the "power of God," who is a "God not of the dead, but of the living" (see Lk 20:27–38). After Easter, the apostles added the *Christological* foundation to the *theological* one: the resurrection of Christ from the dead. The apostle established faith in the resurrection of the flesh and life everlasting on the resurrection of Christ: "Now if Christ is proclaimed as raised from the dead, how can some of you say there is no resurrection of the dead? But in fact Christ has been raised from the dead, the first fruits of those who have died" (1 Cor 15:12, 20).

Even in the Greco-Roman world, an evolution in the concept of the afterlife took place. The most primitive belief was that true life ended in death; afterward they believed only in a wormlike existence in a world of shadows. Something new took place with the appearance in Greece of the Orphic-Pythagorean religion in the sixth century BC.* According to it, the true self of humanity was the soul, which, once freed from the prison (*sema*) of the body (*soma*), could finally live its true life. Plato gave this development a philosophical dignity, basing it on the spiritual, and therefore immortal, nature of the soul.2

This belief, however, would remain for the most part in the minority, reserved to those who were initiated in mysteries or were followers of particular schools of philosophy. For the masses, the ancient belief persisted that true life ended at death. The words that Emperor Hadrian addressed to himself on his deathbed are well-known:

> Small soul, lost and gentle,
> companion and host of my body,

---

* Orphic-Pythagorean religion originated in Greece around the sixth century BC and stressed the separation of soul and body. *Ed.*

now hurry to ascend to places
colorless, arduous, and bare
where you will no longer have your usual pleasures.
For one more moment,
let's look along the familiar shores
at the things we shall certainly never see again.[3]

Against this background, it is easy to understand the impact that the Christian proclamation of life after death must have had, a life infinitely fuller and more joyous than the earthly one. It is also understandable why the idea and symbols of everlasting life are so common in the Christian sepulchers in the catacombs.

But what has become of the Christian idea of everlasting life for the soul and the body, after it triumphed over the pagan idea of "shadows after death?" In the nineteenth century atheism tended to express itself in denial of the afterlife, as opposed to today in which atheism is primarily expressed in denial of the existence of a Creator. Taking up Hegel's claim, according to which "Christians waste in heaven the energies destined for earth," Feuerbach and especially Marx fought above all against belief in life after death, under the pretext that it alienates people from their earthly commitment. The idea of personal survival in God is replaced with the idea of survival of the species and of future society. Little by little, the word "eternity" has fallen into oblivion and silence and is now met with suspicion. Materialism and consumerism have done the rest in affluent societies, making it unbecoming to continue to speak of eternity among educated people who are in step with the times.

All of this has had clear repercussions on the faith of believers who have become timid and reticent on this issue. When is the last time you heard a sermon preached on eternal life? We continue to recite in the Creed, "I look forward to the resurrection of the dead and the life of the world to come," but without giving much weight to the words. Kierkegaard was right when he wrote: "The afterlife has become a joke, a need so uncertain that not only does no one respect it any longer, but neither do they hope for it any longer, to the point that it seems amusing even to think that there was once a time when this idea transformed the whole of existence."4

What is the practical consequence of this eclipse of belief in eternity? Saint Paul refers to the purpose of those who do not believe in resurrection from the dead, "Let us eat and drink, for tomorrow we die" (1 Cor 15:32). The natural desire to live *forever*, if distorted, can become a desire, even a frenzy, to live *well*, that is, in pleasure, even at the expense of others, if necessary. The entire earth becomes what Dante said of Italy at his time, *"l'aiuola che ci fa tanto feroci"* ("this little plot of ground that makes us so ferocious").5 Having lost the outlook of eternity, human suffering appears doubly and irreparably absurd.

3. Longing for eternity

The most effective response to secularism, as for scientism, does not necessarily consist in combating the error. Instead, it consists in making the assurance of eternal life shine anew before humanity and by appealing to the inherent force that truth possesses when it is accompanied by the witness of one's life. An ancient Father wrote, "One can always oppose an idea with another idea and an opinion with another opinion; but with what can one oppose a life?"

We must also bring out the deepest desire, even if repressed, of the human heart that corresponds to such truth. Miguel de Unamuno (no apologist for the faith) responded in a letter to a friend who reproached him for his longing for eternity, as if it were a form of pride and presumption:

> I am not saying that we merit an afterlife, nor that logic proves it; I am saying that we need it whether or not we deserve it. That's all. I am saying that what passes does not satisfy me, and I thirst for eternity. Without this, everything is indifferent to me. I need it, I need it! Without it, there is no longer any joy of life, and the joy of living has nothing left to say to me. It is too easy to claim: "We must live, we must be content with life." Then what of those who are not content with it?[6]

On the same occasion he added that it is not the person who desires eternity who shows contempt for the world and life here below, but rather those who do not desire it: "I so love life that to lose it seems to me the worst of evils. Those do not really love life who enjoy it, day after day, without bothering to know whether or not they will lose it completely or not." Saint Augustine said the same thing, "What good is it to live well, if it is not given to live forever?"[7] "Everything, except eternity, is vain to the world," an Italian poet sang.[8] To those of our age who cultivate this need of eternity within the profundity of their hearts, without perhaps having the courage to even admit it to themselves, we can repeat what Paul said to the Athenians, "What therefore you worship as unknown, this I proclaim to you" (Acts 17:23).

The Christian response to secularism (in the sense we understand it here) is not based, as it is for Plato, on a philosophical idea—the immortality of the soul—but on an event. The Enlightenment posed the crucial question of how one could attain eternity while in time, and how one could give a point of departure within history for an eternal consciousness.[9] In other words, how can one justify the Christian faith's claim that promises eternal life and equally threatens eternal punishment for acts committed in time? The only acceptable response to this problem is one based on faith in the Incarnation of God. In Christ, the Eternal entered into time and was revealed in the flesh; in him, it is possible to make a decision based on eternity. This is how John the Evangelist speaks of eternal life, "we have seen it and testify to it, and declare to you the eternal life that was with the Father and was revealed to us" (1 Jn 1:2).

4. Eternity: a hope and a presence

For the believer, eternity is not, as we can see, only a hope; it is also a presence. We experience this every time we make a true act of faith in Christ, for whoever believes in him already has eternal life (see 1 Jn 5:13); every time we receive Communion, because in it "we are given the guarantee of future glory"; every time we hear the words of the Gospel, which are the "words of eternal life" (Jn 6:68). Saint Thomas Aquinas said that "grace is already the beginning of glory." [10]

The presence of eternity in time is called the Holy Spirit. He is defined as "the pledge of our inheritance" (Eph 1:14; see 2 Cor 5:5). He was given to us so that, after having received the first fruits, we might yearn for the fullness. Saint Augustine wrote: "Christ has given us the guarantee of the Holy Spirit with which he, who in any case could not deceive us, wanted to render us certain of the fulfillment of his promise. What did he promise? He promised eternal life of which the Spirit, which he gave us, is the guarantee." [11]

The relationship between the life of faith in time and eternal life is analogous to the relationship between the life of the embryo in a mother's womb and the child after birth. Cabasilas writes:

This world bears in gestation the inner man, new, created according to God, until he, molded here, modeled and made perfect, is generated in that perfect world that does not grow old. Just as the embryo which, while it is in its dark and fluid existence, nature prepares for life in the light, so it is with the saints. . . . For the embryo, however, the future life is absolutely the future; no ray of light reaches it, there is nothing of what is of this life. Not so for us, from the moment that the future age was poured and mingled with this present one. . . . Because of this, it is already granted to saints not only to dispose and prepare themselves for life, but to live and operate in it.[12]

The following story illustrates this comparison. Once there were twins—a boy and a girl—who were so intelligent and precocious that they already spoke to one another even in their mother's womb. The girl asked her brother, "Do you think there will be life after birth?" He replied, "Don't be ridiculous. What makes you think there is something outside this cramped and dark space in which we find ourselves?" Gathering courage, the girl insisted, "Who knows, maybe there is a mother or perhaps someone who put us here and who will take care of us." He said, "Do you see, perchance, a mother somewhere? What you see is all there is." She said again, "But don't you too sometimes feel a pressure on your chest which increases day by day and is pushing us forward?" "On second thought," the brother responded, "it is true; I do feel it all the time." The sister concluded triumphantly, "Do you see? This pain cannot be for nothing. I think it is preparing us for something greater than this small space."

We can use this little story when we must proclaim eternal life to people who have lost their faith in it, but who retain a longing for it. Perhaps they even expect the Church, like the little girl, to help them become aware of their desire.

5. Who are we? Where do we come from? Where are we going?

The human race has been asking itself these questions since time immemorial, and people today are no exception: "Who are we? Where do we come from? Where are we going?" In *The Ecclesiastical History of the English People*, the Venerable Bede recounts how the Christian faith came to Northern England. When missionaries from Rome arrived in Northumberland, King Edwin called a council of dignitaries to decide whether or not to allow them to spread their new message. One of them stood up and said:

> The present life of man, O king, seems to me, in comparison with that time which is unknown to us, like to the swift flight of a sparrow through the room wherein you sit at supper in winter amid your officers and ministers, with a good fire in the midst, whilst the storms of rain and snow prevail abroad; the sparrow, I say, flying in at one door and immediately out at another, whilst he is within is safe from the wintry storm; but after a short space of fair weather he immediately vanishes out of your sight into the dark winter from which he has emerged. So this life of man appears for a short space, but of what went before or what is to follow we are utterly ignorant. If, therefore, this new doctrine contains something more certain, it seems justly to deserve to be followed.13

Perhaps the Christian faith will return to England and to the Western secularized world for the same reason that it made its entrance: as the only one that offers certain answers to the great questions of life on earth. The most favorable occasion to convey this message is at funerals. Here, people are less distracted than during other rites of passage (baptism, marriage, and so on), and they are often wondering about their own destiny. Those who weep over their deceased loved ones also weep for themselves. Saint Augustine, while writing about the death of his mother, Monica, said that he wept "over her and for her, over me and for me."14

I once heard an interesting program on so-called "secular" or "humanist funerals," with a live broadcast of one of them. At one point, the officiant said to those present, "We should not be sad. To live a good, fulfilling life of seventy-eight years [the age of the deceased] is something for which we should be grateful." Grateful to whom, I wondered. Such a funeral only makes the total defeat of humanity in the face of death all the more apparent.

The opportunity for evangelization at funerals can be damaged in two ways. Sometimes ministers lack a genuine sense of humanity and have no interest in the deceased; they cannot weep like Jesus did before of the pain of others. Other times, the minister does not go beyond the level of human pleasantries and lacks the courage to announce the good news of Christ's victory over death.

Cardinal Newman helps us to complete our reflections with a truth hitherto unmentioned. He does so in his poem, *The Dream of Gerontius*, set to music by the English composer Edward Elgar. It was a true masterpiece for its depth of thoughts, lyrical inspiration, liturgical choral music, and drama.

Newman describes the dream of an old man who feels he is near death, but we know he is actually dealing with himself at a particular time in his life. His thoughts on the meaning of life, death, and the abyss of nothingness into which he is falling are set against the comments of the assistants, the praying voice of the Church: "Go forth upon thy journey, Christian soul" (*proficiscere, anima christiana*), and the conflicting voices of angels and demons that burden his life and claim his soul. The moment of his transition from time into eternity is described with very effective images:

I feel in me an inexpressive lightness, and a sense
Of freedom, as I were at length myself
And ne'er had been before. How still it is!
I hear no more the busy beat of time,
No, nor my fluttering breath, nor struggling pulse;
Nor does one moment differ from the next.[15]

The last words spoken by the soul in the poem are those with which he sets out serenely, even impatiently, to Purgatory:

"There will I sing my absent Lord and Love:
Take me away,
That sooner I may rise, and go above,
And see Him in the truth of everlasting day."[16]

For Emperor Hadrian, as we have read, death was a transition from reality to the shadows; for the Christian, John Newman, it is the transition from shadows to reality. *Ex umbris et imaginibus in veritatem* ["from shadows and images into truth"] was the inscription he wished to have written on his tomb.

What, then, is the truth that Newman obliges us to be open about? That the transition from time to eternity is not straight and equal for all. We must face a judgment, which can have two very different outcomes: hell or heaven. Newman's spirituality is austere, almost rigorous at times; it recalls that of "*Dies Irae*," the "Day of Wrath" written by Thomas of Celano. "Along my earthly life," the soul of Gerontius says to his guardian angel, "the thought of death and judgment was to me most terrible. I had it aye before me, and I saw the Judge severe e'en in the Crucifix." But for this reason, it can be a useful corrective tool in an age inclined to take the thought of eternity lightly or as a joke, as Kierkegaard said.

In our secularized Western world, some people think that reincarnation can provide a way to escape the terrible seriousness of life and death. This doctrine, however, is incompatible with Christian faith in the resurrection. Furthermore, in the way reincarnation is popularized in our culture, it is the result of a gross misunderstanding. In the original context in which the doctrine was born (and is still professed), it is not intended as a means of enjoying life longer but as an extension of suffering. It is not a motive of consolation but of fear. It is a threat and a punishment. It is like saying to a prisoner who has come near the end of his prison term that his sentence has just been doubled and he has to start all over again. We have adapted the doctrine of reincarnation to our hedonistic and materialistic Western mentality and transformed it into something completely different. Scripture warns sternly, "it is appointed for mortals to die once [*semel* in Latin], and after that the judgment" (Heb 9:27).

Also due to the uniqueness of human life some have, unfortunately, drawn a conclusion diametrically opposed to the Christian faith. This conclusion has been popularized by the novel, *The Unbearable Lightness of Being*, by the Czech writer Milan Kundera. In agreement with the German proverb, *einmal ist keinmal* ("what happens only once is like it never happened"), the author affirms the total irrelevance of human existence as if it were a dress rehearsal for a performance that will never take place. Without previous lives to learn from or future lives in which to practice what we have learned, the choices we make appear insignificant—and here is their "lightness"; this makes any attempt to give meaning to life an "unbearable" effort.[17]

According to the Christian faith, it is precisely the fact that one lives just once (*semel, einmal*), that human life has its great "depth" and its extraordinary relevance! It is true that we do not have prior lives to learn from and future lives on earth in which to atone, but we have many things from which we can learn how to live: natural law, the experience of others, our own experiences—life does not last only one day! Then, for those who believe, there is the Word of God and especially the life of a man like us, Jesus of Nazareth.

6. Go to the house of the Lord!

A renewed hope in eternity does not serve only for evangelization, that is, for the proclamation made to others. Even before that, it serves to revitalize our own journey toward holiness. The weakening of belief in eternity also affects believers, lessening in them the ability to courageously face suffering and the trials of life. We are no longer accustomed, like Saint Bernard and Saint Ignatius of Loyola, to ask before every situation, "*Quid hoc aeternitatem?*" ("What good is this for eternity?").

Let us consider a man who is holding a lever scale—one of those old-fashioned handheld balances. On one side, it has a plate on which to place items to be weighed, while on the other side it has a graduated arm to hold the weights. If the weights come off, everything on the plate will make the bar go up and tilt the scale down on the side of the plate. Anything—even a handful of feathers—would have the upper hand.

This is how we are when we lose the measure of everything that is of eternity: worldly things and sufferings can easily beat down our souls. Everything seems for us too heavy, too excessive. Jesus said:

> "If your hand or your foot causes you to stumble, cut it off and throw it away; it is better for you to enter life maimed or lame than to have two hands or two feet and to be thrown into the eternal fire. And if your eye causes you to stumble, tear it out and throw it away; it is better for you to enter life with one eye than to have two eyes and to be thrown into the hell of fire." (Mt 18:8–9)

But having lost sight of eternity, we find it excessive to even be asked to close our eyes during an immoral program.

Saint Paul dares to write: "For this slight momentary affliction is preparing us for an eternal weight of glory beyond all measure, because we look not at what can be seen but at what cannot be seen; for what can be seen is temporary, but what cannot be seen is eternal" (2 Cor 4:17–18). The weight of the affliction is "slight" precisely because it is temporary; that of glory is beyond all measure because it is eternal. This is why the same apostle can say, "I consider that the sufferings of this present time are not worth comparing with the glory about to be revealed to us" (Rom 8:18).

The Hebrew Psalter contains a group of psalms known as the "psalms of ascent," or the "Songs of Zion." They were the canticles that the Israelite pilgrims sang when they "went up" on pilgrimage to the holy city of Jerusalem. One of them begins, "I was glad when they said to me, 'Let us go to the house of the LORD!'" (Ps 122:1). These psalms of ascent have now become the psalms of those in the Church who are journeying toward the heavenly Jerusalem. They are our psalms. Commenting on the initial words of the psalm just quoted, Saint Augustine said to his followers:

> Let us run because we will go to the house of the Lord. Let us run and not grow weary because this course does not exhaust us; because we will arrive at an end where there is no weariness. Let us run to the house of the Lord, and our soul rejoices for those who repeat these words. They have seen the homeland before us; the Apostles saw it and said to us: "Run, hurry up, follow us! We are going to the house of the Lord."[18]

In the face of every difficulty and problem, we can repeat with Saint Bernard, "*Quid hoc aeternitatem?*" ("What good is this for eternity?"). And we can also repeat with the poet Fogazzaro, "Everything, except eternity, is vain to the world."

Notes

Chapter 1: Go into All the World

1. Adolf von Harnack, *Mission und Die Ausbreitung des Christentums in den ersten drei Jahrhunderten* [*The Mission and Expansion of Christianity in the First Three Centuries*] (Leipzig: Hinrichs, 1902).

2. Origen, *Contra Celsum*, Book III, chap. 9. Trans. Frederick Crombie, *Ante-Nicene Fathers, Vol. 4*, ed. Alexander Roberts, James Donaldson, and A. Cleveland Coxe (Buffalo, NY: Christian Literature Publishing Co., 1885). Courtesy of Christian Classics Ethereal Library (CCEL), http://www.ccel.org/ccel/schaff/anf04.vi.ix.iii.ix.html.

3. Harnack, *The Mission and Expansion of Christianity in the First Three Centuries*. Trans. by James Moffatt (London: Williams & Norgate, 1908), Book III, chap. IV. Courtesy of CCEL, http://www.ccel.org/ccel/harnack/mission.txt.

4. See Henry Chadwick, *The Early Church* (Harmondsworth: Penguin Books, 1967), 56–58.

5. Harnack, *Mission and Expansion*, op. cit., book II, chap. VI. The Latin Vulgate text is *"rationabile obsequium,"* which can be translated "reasonable worship." The author cites the Italian Scripture here in its Latinate form.

6. Harnack, *Mission and Expansion*, book III, chap. V.

7. Søren Kierkegaard, *Diario*, X5 A 98 [*The Diary of Soren Kierkegaard*], ed. C. Fabro, II (Brescia: Morcelliana, 1963), 386ff. FSP translation.

8. Saint Justin Martyr, *First Apology*. From *Ante-Nicene Fathers, Vol. 1*, ed. Alexander Roberts, James Donaldson, and A. Cleveland Coxe (Buffalo, NY: Christian Literature Publishing Co., 1885; reprinted by William B. Eerdmans Publishing Company, 2001), *The First Apology*, Chap. II. Courtesy CCEL, http://www.ccel.org/ccel/schaff/anf01.viii.ii.ii.html.

9. Pope Paul VI, "*Udienza Generale in Insegnamenti di Paolo VI*," X, Tipografia Poliglotta Vaticana, Città del Vaticano 1972, 1210s, [Papal Audience Address, November 29, 1972], http://www.vatican.va/holy_father/paul_vi/audiences/1972/documents/hf_p-vi_aud_19721129_it.html. FSP translation.

10. Charles Péguy, *Il Portico del Mistero della Seconda Virtù* [*Portico of the Mystery of the Second Virtue*] (Milan: Jaca Book, 1978), 120s. FSP translation.

Chapter 2: There Is No Longer Greek or Jew, Barbarian or Scythian

1. Saint Jerome, *Commentary on Ezekiel*, Preface to Book III, PL 25, 75, cf. le *Epist.* LX, 16; CXXIII, 15–16; CXXVI, 2 (PL 22, 600.1057.1086). From *Nicene and Post-Nicene Fathers, Series II, Volume 6*, Preface to Book III, ed. Philip Schaff and trans. The Hon. W. H. Freemantle, M.A. (New York: Christian Literature Publishing, Co., 1892), 1084. Courtesy CCEL, http://www.ccel.org/ccel/schaff/npnf206.vii.iv.x.html.

2. Saint Leo the Great, *Sermon 82, 1*. From *Nicene and Post-Nicene Fathers, Series II, Volume 12*, ed. Philip Schaff and trans. Rev. Charles Lett Feltoe, M.A. (New York: Christian Literature Publishing, Co., 1892), 514. Courtesy CCEL, http://www.ccel.org/ccel/schaff/npnf212.ii.v.xlii.html.

3. Saint Gregory of Tours, *Historia Francorum*, Book II, 31 (PL 71, 227). The Sigambri were the tribe of Gauls from which Clovis descended. FSP translation.

4. John Paul II, *Redemptoris Missio* (Boston: Pauline Books & Media, 1990), no. 55.

5. Vatican Council II, *Decree Ad Gentes* (Boston: Pauline Books & Media, 1965), no. 18.

6. John Paul II, "*Discorso di Giovanni Paolo II Alle Suore di Clausura nel Monastero Dell'incarnazione ad Avila*" [Address on the Conclusion of the Fourth Centenary of the Death of St. Teresa of Jesus], http://www.vatican.va/holy_father/john_paul_ii/speeches/ 1982/november/ documents/hf_jp-ii_spe_19821101_suore-clausura-avila_it.html. November 1, 1982. FSP translation.

7. *Legend of Perugia*, 80, taken from *Saint Francis of Assisi Writings and Early Biographies: English Omnibus of the Sources for the Life of Saint Francis* edited by Marion Alphonse Habig (Chicago: Franciscan Herald Press, 1983), 1056.

8. Origen, *Commentary on the Gospel of John*, I, 6, 23 (SCh 120, 70), from *Ante-Nicene Fathers*, Vol. 9 ed. Philip Schaff (New York: Christian Literature Publishing, Co., 1885). Courtesy of CCEL, http://www.ccel.org/ccel/schaff/anf09.xv.iii.i.vi.html.

9. Pope Paul VI, *Evangelii Nuntiandi: On Evangelization in the Modern World* (Boston: Pauline Books & Media, 1976), no. 82.

Chapter 3: To the Ends of the Earth

1. See J. Glazik in *Storia della Chiesa*, ed. H. Jedin, vol. VI (Milan: Jaca Book, 1975), 702.

2. See Francis Sullivan, SJ, *Salvation Outside the Church? Tracing the History of the Catholic Response* (New York: Paulist Press, 1992), 69–75.

3. John Paul II, "*Discurso del Santo Padre Juan Pablo II a los Participantes en el Simposio Internacional Sobre la Historia de la Evangelización de América*" [To the Participants of the International Symposium on the History of Evangelization in America], no. 3, May 14, 1992, http://www.vatican.va/holy_father/john_paul_ii/speeches/ 1992/may/documents/hf_jp-ii_spe_19920514_simposium-evangeli-zacion_sp.html. FSP translation.

4. See Glazik, cit., 708.

5. Pope Paul VI, "Address to the International Conference on the Catholic Charismatic Renewal," May 19, 1975. FSP translation.

6. John Paul II, *Los caminos del Evangelio*, June 29, 1990, no. 24. http://www.vatican.va/holy_father/john_paul_ii/apost_letters/documents/hf_jp-ii_apl_29061990_v-centenary-evang-new-world_sp. html. FSP translation.

7. John Paul II, "Apostolic Letter: A Concilio Constantinopolitano I," March 25, 1981, no. 7, http://www.vatican.va/holy_father/john_paul_ii/apost_letters/documents/hf_jp-ii_apl_25031981_a-concilio-constantinopolitano-i_ en.html.

8. Saint Bonaventura, *"Sermone per la IV Domenica dopo Pasqua, 2"* [Sermon for the Fourth Sunday after Easter], 2, ed. Quaracchi, IX (Florence, 1901), 311. FSP translation.

Chapter 4: Starting from the Beginning

1. Pope Benedict XVI, "Apostolic Letter in the Form of Motu Proprio, *Ubicumque et Semper*," September 21, 2010. http://www.vatican.va/holy_father/benedict_xvi/apost_letters/documents/hf_ben-xvi_apl_20100921_ubicumque-et-semper_en.html.

2. Pope Paul VI, "Constitution on the Sacred Liturgy, *Sacrosanctum Concilium*" (December 4, 1963), no. 7. http://www.vatican.va/archive/hist_councils/ii_vatican_council/documents/vat-ii_const_19631204_sacrosanctum-concilium_en.html.

3. Cf. Charles Péguy, *Le Mystère des Saints Innocents* (Paris: Gallimard, 1975), 697.

4. Søren Kierkegaard, *Training in Christianity*, trans. Walter Lowrie, pref. Richard John Neuhaus (New York: Random House, 2004), 29.

5. Easter Homilies of the year 387 (SCh 36, 59s) [Cantalamessa does not cite the author.] FSP translation.

6. Pope Paul VI, *Dogmatic Constitution on the Church: Lumen Gentium* (Boston: Pauline Books & Media, 1965), no. 12.

7. Pope Benedict XVI, "Address to the Plenary Assembly of the Pontifical Council for the Family," December 1, 2011. http://www.

vatican.va/holy_father/benedict_xvi/speeches/2011/december/documents/hf_ben-xvi_spe_20111201_pc-family_en.html.

8. Saint Leo the Great, *"Discorso 6 per il Natale"* ["Sermon 6 for Christmas"] 2 (PL 54, 213s). FSP translation.

9. Origen, *Commento al Vangelo di Luca [Commentary on the Gospel of Luke]* 22, 3 (SCh 87, 302). FSP translation.

Chapter 5: "What Are Human Beings That You Are Mindful of Them?"

1. John Paul II, *Fides et Ratio* (Boston: Pauline Books & Media, 1998), no. 88.

2. Jacques Monod, *Il caso e la necessità* [*Chance and Necessity*] (Milan: Mondadori, 1970), 136s. FSP translation.

3. Stephen Hawking, *The Grand Design* (New York: Bantam Books, 2010), 180.

4. M. Planck, *La conoscenza del mondo fisico* (Turin: Bollati Boringhieri, 1993), 155, quoted by R.Timossi, *L'illusione dell'ateismo. Perché la scienza non nega Dio* (San Paolo: Cinisello Balsamo 2009, 160). FSP translation.

5. See, e.g., the detailed criticism by Timossi, *L'illusione dell'ateismo*, op. cit.

6. John Henry Newman, "Letter to John Walker" (1868), in *The Letters and Diaries of John Henry Cardinal Newman: Vol. XXIV: A Grammar of Assent. January 1868 to December 1869* (Oxford: Clarendon Press, 1973), 77ff.

7. John Henry Newman, *Apologia pro vita sua* (London: Longman, Green, and Co., 1865), chap 5. Courtesy of the Newman Reader (NR), http://www.newmanreader.org/works/apologia65/chapter5.html.

8. John Henry Newman, *An Essay on the Development of Christian Doctrine* (London: Longman, Green, and Co., 1909), Sec. 2, 4. Courtesy of the NR, http://www.newmanreader.org/works/development/chapter2.html.

9. Monod, *Chance and Necessity*, op. cit.

10. P. Atkins, quoted by Timossi, *L'illusione dell'ateismo*, op. cit., 482. FSP translation.

11. Blaise Pascal, *Pensieri*, 347 (ed. Brunschwicg). FSP translation.

12. M. Blondel and A. Valensin, *Correspondance* (Paris: Aubier, 1957), 47. FSP translation.

13. In Origen, *Contra Celsum*, IV, 23 (SCh 136, 238); cf. also IV, 74 (SCh 136, 366). Courtesy of CCEL, http://www.ccel.org/ccel/schaff/anf04.vi.ix.iv.xxiii.html.

14. Cf. M. Pohlenz, *L'uomo greco* (Milan: Bompiani, 2006).

15. In Origen, *Contra Celsum*, IV, 30 (SCh 136, 254). Courtesy of CCEL, http://www.ccel.org/ccel/schaff/anf04.vi.ix.iv.xxx.html.

16. *Scolii* a Dionigi Areopagita (PG 4, 536); cf. Dionigi Areopagita, *Lettera* VI (PG 3, 1077). FSP translation.

17. G. Bardy, *Dictionnaire de spiritualité, ascétique et mystique*, vol. III (Paris: Beauchesne, 1937), col. 1389ff. FSP translation.

18. Saint Leo the Great, "Sermon 1 on Christmas" (PL 54, 190s). Translation courtesy of the *Catechism of the Catholic Church*, no. 1691.

19. Dialogue with Motovilov, in I. Gorainoff, *Serafino di Sarov* (Turin: Gribaudi, 1981), 156. FSP translation.

20. Saint Athanasius, *The Incarnation of the Lord*, 54 (PG 25, 192B). FSP translation.

21. Saint Gregory Nazianus, *Discorsi teologici*, III, 19 (PG 36, 100A). FSP translation.

22. J. Ratzinger, *Introduction to Christianity* (San Francisco: Ignatius Press, 2004), 141.

Chapter 6: "Always Be Ready to Make Your Defense to Anyone Who Demands an Accounting from You"

1. John Henry Newman, *Oxford University Sermons* (London: Longman, Green, and Co., 1909), Sermon 5, par. 26. Courtesy of the NR: http://www.newmanreader.org/works/oxford/sermon5.html.

2. Ibid. Preface, par. 11. Courtesy of the NR: http://www.newmanreader.org/works/oxford/index.html.

3. Ibid. Sermon 10, par. 14. Courtesy of the NR: http://www.newmanreader.org/works/oxford/sermon10.html.

4. Ibid. Sermon 10, par. 15.

5. Pascal, *Pensieri*, cit., 267. FSP translation.

6. Saint Augustine, Epist. 130, 28 (PL 33, 505). FSP translation.

7. Kierkegaard, *The Diary of Soren Kierkegaard*, VIII A 11. FSP translation.

8. Newman, *Oxford University Sermons*, op. cit., 262, Sermon 13, par. 15. Courtesy of the NR: http://www.newmanreader.org/works/oxford/sermon13.html.

9. Pascal, *Pensieri*, op. cit., 277. FSP translation.

10. R. Otto, Das Heilige, *Über das Irrationale in der Idee des Göttlichen und sein Verhältnis zum Rationalen* (Breslau: Trewendt & Granier, 1917). English edition: *The Idea of the Holy*, trans. John W. Harvey (London: H. Milford, Oxford University Press, 1923).

11. Saint Augustine, *Confessions*, bk. VII, chap. 10, Confessions and Enchiridion, trans. and ed. Albert C. Outler from the Library of Christian Classics, V. 7 (Philadelphia: Westminster Press, 1955). Courtesy of CCEL: http://www.ccel.org/ccel/augustine/confessions/confessions.html.

12. Ibid., bk. XI, chap. 9.

13. Immanuel Kant, *Critica della ragion pratica* [*Critique of Practical Reason and Other Works on the Theory of Ethics*], trans. Thomas Kingsmill Abbott, B.D. (London: Longmans, Green, and Co., 1889), 260.

14. F. Collins, *The Language of God: A Scientist Presents Evidence for Belief* (New York: Free Press, 2006), 219, 255.

15. Clement of Alexandria, *Stromata*, 2, 9 [Clement is quoting from the apocryphal *Gospel to the Hebrews. Ed.*]. FSP translation.

16. Fyodor Dostoyevsky, *The Brothers Karamazov*, trans. Constance Garnett (New York : Lowell, 1900), 331.

17. Giacomo Leopardi, "The Infinite" in *The Poems of Leopardi*, trans. Francis Henry Cliffe (London: Remington and Co., Ltd., 1893), 92.

18. Dionysius the Areopagite, *Divine Names,* chap. II, sec. 9, *pati divina.* FSP translation.

19. This is what E. Zola does in his well-known anthology: *I mistici dell'occidente,* vol. 7 (Milan: Mondadori, 1980).

20. Karl Rahner, *Theological Investigations,* 7 (London: Dartman, Longman, and Todd, 1974), 15. FSP translation.

21. Newman, *Oxford University Sermons,* op. cit., 91–92, Sermon 5 par. 26. Courtesy of the NR: http://www.newmanreader.org/works/oxford/sermon5.html.

22. Pope Paul VI, *Evangelii Nuntiandi* (Boston: Pauline Books & Media, 1975), no. 41.

23. Saint Gregory Nazianus, *Carmina,* XXIX. FSP translation.

Chapter 7: We Have Seen and Testify to It, and Declare to You Eternal Life

1. Benedict XVI, "Apostolic Letter in the Form of *Motu Proprio, Ubicumque et Semper,*" September 21, 2010, art. 2.

2. Cf. Pohlenz, *L'uomo greco,* op. cit., 173ff.

3. *Animula vagula, blandula,* cit. in M. Yourcenar, *Memorie di Adriano,* L. Storoni Mazzolani (Turin: Einaudi, 1988). FSP translation.

4. S. Kierkegaard, *Postilla conclusiva,* vol. 4, in *Opere,* ed. C. Fabro (Florence: Sansoni, 1972), 458. FSP translation.

5. Dante Alighieri, *The Divine Comedy,* Paradise XXII, 151. FSP translation.

6. Miguel de Unamuno, "*Cartas inéditas de Miguel de Unamuno y Pedro Jiménez Ilundain,*" ed. Hernán Benítez, *Journal of the University of Buenos Aires,* vol. 3, no. 9 (1949), 135.150. FSP translation.

7. Saint Augustine, *Tractates on the Gospel of John,* 45, 2. FSP translation.

8. A. Fogazzaro, "A Sera," in *Le poesie* (Milan: Mondadori, 1935), 194–197. FSP translation.

9. See G. E. Lessing, *Über den Beweis des Geistes und der Kraft,* in *Sämtliche Schriften,* ed. K. Lachmann, vol. X (Stuttgart: Göschen, 1838–1840), 36.

10. Saint Thomas Aquinas, *Summa Theologiae*, II–II, q. 24, art. 3, ad 2. FSP translation.

11. Saint Augustine, *Sermons* 378, 1. FSP translation.

12. N. Cabasilas, *Vita in Cristo*, I, 1–2, ed. U. Neri (Turin: UTET, 1971), 65–67. FSP translation.

13. Venerable Bede, *Ecclesiastical History of the English People*, II, 13 (PL 95, 104) as found in *Readings in European History: A Collection of Extracts from the Sources Chosen with the Purpose of Illustrating the Progress of Culture in Western Europe Since the German Invasions* by James Harvey Robinson (Boston: Ginn and Company, 1906), 52–53.

14. Saint Augustine, *Confessions,* XII, 33. FSP translation.

15. John Henry Newman, *"The Dream of Gerontius"* in *Verses on Various Occasions* (London: Longman, Green, and Co., 1903), 323. Courtesy of the NR: http://www.newmanreader.org/works/verses/gerontius.html.

16. Ibid.

17. See Milan Kundera, *The Unbearable Lightness of Being.*

18. Saint Augustine, *Enarrationes in Psalmos,* 121, 2. FSP translation.

RANIERO CANTALAMESSA, OFM CAP., was appointed by Pope John Paul II Preacher to the Papal Household in 1980 and has continued to serve in this capacity during the papacies of both Pope Benedict XVI and Pope Francis. He holds two doctorates (in divinity and classical literature) as well as several honorary degrees. Father Cantalamessa has published numerous books on theology and spirituality, which have been translated into more than twenty languages. When he is not engaged in preaching, he lives in a hermitage at Cittaducale (Rieti), Italy, ministering to a small community of cloistered nuns.

BOOKS & MEDIA

The Daughters of St. Paul operate book and media centers at the following addresses. Visit, call, or write the one nearest you today, or find us at www.pauline.org.

California
3908 Sepulveda Blvd, Culver City, CA 90230310-397-8676
935 Brewster Avenue, Redwood City, CA 94063650-369-4230
5945 Balboa Avenue, San Diego, CA 92111858-565-9181

Florida
145 S.W. 107th Avenue, Miami, FL 33174305-559-6715

Hawaii
1143 Bishop Street, Honolulu, HI 96813808-521-2731
Neighbor Islands call:866-521-2731

Illinois
172 North Michigan Avenue, Chicago, IL 60601312-346-4228

Louisiana
4403 Veterans Memorial Blvd, Metairie, LA 70006504-887-7631

Massachusetts
885 Providence Hwy, Dedham, MA 02026781-326-5385

Missouri
9804 Watson Road, St. Louis, MO 63126314-965-3512

New York
64 W. 38th Street, New York, NY 10018212-754-1110

Pennsylvania
Philadelphia—relocating215-676-9494

South Carolina
243 King Street, Charleston, SC 29401843-577-0175

Virginia
1025 King Street, Alexandria, VA 22314703-549-3806

Canada
3022 Dufferin Street, Toronto, ON M6B 3T5416-781-9131

¡También somos su fuente para libros, videos y música en español!